The Idea of the American University

The Idea of the American University

Edited by
Bradley C. S. Watson

LEXINGTON BOOKS

A division of

ROWMAN & LITTLEFIELD PUBLISHERS, INC.
Lanham • Boulder • New York • Toronto • Plymouth, UK

Published by Lexington Books
A division of Rowman & Littlefield Publishers, Inc.
A wholly owned subsidiary of The Rowman & Littlefield Publishing Group, Inc.
4501 Forbes Boulevard, Suite 200, Lanham, Maryland 20706
http://www.lexingtonbooks.com

Estover Road, Plymouth PL6 7PY, United Kingdom

British Library Cataloguing in Publication Information Available

Library of Congress Cataloging-in-Publication Data

The idea of the American university / edited by Bradley C. S. Watson.
   p. cm.
   ISBN 978-0-7391-4915-7 (cloth : alk. paper) — ISBN 978-0-7391-4917-1 (electronic)
   1. Universities and colleges—United States. 2. Education, Higher—United
States. 3. Education, Higher—Aims and objectives—United States. I. Watson,
Bradley C. S., 1961–
   LA227.4.I335 2011
   378.73—dc22   2010048636

♾ ™ The paper used in this publication meets the minimum requirements of American
National Standard for Information Sciences—Permanence of Paper for Printed Library
Materials, ANSI/NISO Z39.48-1992.

Printed in the United States of America

For the students and teachers of universal knowledge

Knowledge is capable of being its own end. Such is the constitution of the human mind, that any kind of knowledge, if it be really such, is its own reward.

—John Henry Newman

Contents

Acknowledgments

This book is based on papers presented by leading thinkers and educators at a conference held at Saint Vincent College in Latrobe, Pennsylvania. The conference was sponsored by the Center for Political and Economic Thought, an interdisciplinary public affairs institute of Saint Vincent's Alex G. McKenna School of Business, Economics, and Government. The Center combines the resources of the college's political science and economics departments. It was founded in 1991 to sponsor research and educational programs in politics, economics, and culture. It seeks to advance a free and well-ordered society in the American and Western traditions.

We at the Center are grateful to Saint Vincent College as a whole for providing a wonderful environment for our biennial Culture and Policy Conferences, as well as our other lectures and conferences—all of which deal with the conditions necessary for a free and decent political, social, economic, and moral order. The Benedictine Order did much to preserve and transmit classical learning and thereby lay the foundations for Western civilization. Saint Vincent, America's first Benedictine college, today remains open and receptive to the conversation about ideas that is so central to that civilization. Special mention should be made of the Rt. Rev. Douglas R. Nowicki, O.S.B., the archabbot of Saint Vincent Archabbey and chancellor of the seminary and the college; Mr. Jim Towey, former president of Saint Vincent College; Br. Norman W. Hipps, O.S.B., the current president of the college; and Dr. John Smetanka, vice president for academic affairs and academic dean of the college.

I have grown accustomed to uttering such words of thanks. I fear I might grow too accustomed and take for granted the rich intellectual soil that the college provides. Saint Vincent is a remarkable institution, and in many ways remains a shimmering beacon on the bleak educational landscape that is described in this book.

I also owe a great deal of thanks to the foundations and individuals that support us. The conference would have been impossible without the confidence and generous support of the Sarah Scaife Foundation and its executive vice president, Michael Gleba. Other conference support was provided by the Philip M. McKenna Foundation, Inc., the Massey Charitable Trust, and the Intercollegiate Studies Institute, Inc.

As a professor at Saint Vincent, I enjoy the college's bounty in numerous ways, prime among them being the support provided by the Center, including especially the friendship of my colleagues therein. I should make special mention of Gary M. Quinlivan, the co-director of the Center and dean of the McKenna School, who never ceases to think of ways to lend energy and aid to our academic projects, and T. William Boxx, the Center's senior fellow, who is a source of good conversation and sound ideas.

I am also indebted to many other individuals who assisted with the conference and book, in ways large and small. Prime among them is Kim Shumaker, the Center's program coordinator, who handled the daunting logistical tasks associated with staging a major academic conference attended by hundreds. Eva Kunkel, assistant to the dean of McKenna School, has provided invaluable aid with many of the tasks associated with publishing this volume. The student staff of the Center aided me in ways too numerous to count.

I am grateful too to the editors and staff at the Rowman & Littlefield Publishing Group and its scholarly imprint, Lexington Books, whose efficient decision and production timelines should be a model for academic publishing.

And of course, I am deeply indebted to the contributors themselves, who remind us of the importance of perhaps the greatest problem, and obligation, we face as political beings—education in the nature of the whole.

I also owe thanks to my wife Barbara and our children, Victoria, Charles, and James—whose futures will be affected profoundly by those who seek to nurture, or destroy, the idea of the American university.

Introduction

The American University in Crisis

Bradley C. S. Watson

Almost everyone who reflects seriously on the American university discerns monumental problems: thinkers who won't teach, teachers who won't think, students who won't learn, administrators who won't leave well enough alone. And as these characters twirl in the satyr play that is American higher education—alternately eliciting gasps and guffaws from the audience—they drag to the stage a seemingly endless list of additional woes: curricular incoherence, fashionable nihilism substituting for genuine thought about the whole, waves of political correctness crashing over the few remaining redoubts of pious and patriotic sentiment, institutional and governmental mandates that make teaching less a vocation than a bureaucratic paper chase. And these are but the tip of the iceberg that underlies the American university and threatens to scuttle even the lifeboats to which a few hardy souls cling.

It is therefore unsurprising that we live in an age of doubt about education, and especially higher education, even as we throw more money at the enterprise. We cannot help but be concerned about what college-educated Americans have been taught—and not taught—about everything from the nature of their constitutional republic to the good life itself.

"Liberal education," "character formation," "civic virtue"—we often associate each of these three human goods, and many others, with the American university. That is to say, they are goods that might, and we tend to think should, be cultivated inside the academy. And, in our most optimistic moments, we can perhaps convince ourselves that they still are. Even those of us of conservative disposition might sometimes fall victim to such bouts of optimism, albeit only briefly; alas for conservatives, optimism is not permitted, but hope springs eternal.

At the very least, it seems likely that we need a coherent idea of the American university in order to ward off despair. This book addresses many questions suggested by such a thought. What is the relationship of the university to those things that transcend human affairs? Whatever happened to the core curriculum, and what does its demise tell us about the idea of the university? What path has the American university followed as it has eschewed serious concern with the things that don't change come what may? Is America eccentric enough to throw up educational institutions that can resist the downforces of modernity? How can liberal education be conceived, much less realized, in an American university that embraces the democratic ethos perhaps more fully than even the regime in which it resides? Can the "liberal arts" ride to the rescue of the American university? Are such arts good or bad for our country, and our souls? Put another way, to what extent are knowledge and virtue—both civic and human—the same?

This volume brings together renowned scholars who have thought broadly and deeply about these and other questions related to the complex enterprise of higher education. The first part of the book, concentrating on the life and times of the American university, opens with Father James V. Schall, who trenchantly asks what it means to have a university without a universe—i.e., a knowable natural order not of our own making, to which, seemingly in a fairy tale, higher education used to be directed. In Schall's apt phrasing, "Modern universities do not study reality. They study themselves explaining the reality that is not there. The only judges they allow are other universities that do the same thing." In abdicating their responsibility to *what is*, they abdicate their responsibility to anything or anyone in particular. They are, in a breathtakingly comprehensive sense, the most irresponsible institutions in America. Contemporary students might escape their bleak nihilism only by chance, or—as it were—by fate.

Each of the remaining chapters in part I offers a distinct perspective on the relativism enucleated by Father Schall. Mark C. Henrie takes on the idea of the core curriculum. In his analysis, universities nowadays might retain watered-down distribution requirements, and a few might even have sensible major requirements, but the core curriculum—a survey of the great intellectual and cultural accomplishments of the West—has all but disappeared. "When all is said and done," according to Henrie, "the demise of the core curriculum is *the* major structural change that separates the curriculum of the 1950s from the curriculum of today." Nonetheless, Henrie cautions that the upheavals of the 1960s have led us to view the American university that antedated that decade through rose-colored lenses. The "traditional" American core curriculum of the first half of the twentieth century differed dramatically from the classical core curriculum that had dominated Western universities from the 16th through the 19th centuries. In the more recent core, by contrast, knowing the classics in their original languages was out, and a certain kind of American instrumental political rationality was in. Consequently, "The Left's charge of indoctrination in the traditional American core curriculum cannot be dispatched as easily as one might wish." Henrie's apologia is not for a political project, or even for the Great Books themselves, understood—courtesy of Allan Bloom—as objects of detached philosophical contemplation. It is rather for great works as a means of accessing the West's common culture and history, with the aim not of liberating but elevating students, while also allowing them to avoid the "parochial clichés of the present age."

In chapter three, Gary D. Glenn uses compelling examples to show just how the American university has fallen into line with Tocqueville's prediction that education in a democracy is bound to concentrate on the pleasures of the body rather than the uplifting of the soul. Glenn attended college at the end of what Henrie describes as the "traditional" period in the history of twentieth century American higher education. According to Glenn, his enforced exposure to the liberal arts made "philosophical thinking a central part of everyone's education. It facilitated and created some commonality of students' intellectual interests. It enabled us go out into the hall of our dorms and engage in a somewhat focused conversation." By enforcing certain intellectual, behavioral, and physical requirements, the university sought to set the conditions for uplifting the souls of its students. In short, it had a comprehensive and serious understanding of its *in loco parentis* responsibilities, for the sake not only of its individual students, but also of both God and country. But as the 60s turned into the 70s and the core curriculum dissolved, intellectual, behavioral, and physical slovenliness crawled ever forward, in tandem, each seemingly parasitic on the others. One might say that at both a philosophical and pre-philosophical level, the university at one time understood the truth of Nietzsche's nostrum that "He who fights with monsters might take care lest he thereby become a monster. And if you gaze for long into an abyss, the abyss gazes also into you." In a theme perhaps common to the writers in this volume, Glenn offers a glimmer of hope to leaven his otherwise somber thoughts. While there are no "systemic solutions" to the crisis of the American university—no plan of action that can recover what has been lost—all is not lost. Hope rests with those—students and teachers—committed to keeping alive the tradition of liberal learning. And, finally, "it depends on such teachers and students finding each other, more or less—but not entirely, as we believe—by chance."

In chapter four, Peter Wood provides a further sense of why genuine human goods that transcend the fashions of the age are so difficult to pursue within the confines of the American university, which "has become too big, too administrative, too diffuse, too fractured, too pluralistic, too unaccountable, too corrupted, too legalistic, and withal too expensive to have a genuine idea of itself. It has instead a marketing plan." In this view, the American university is not so much evil, or even derelict, as it is vulgar, simply uninterested in forming the souls of citizens, who in turn would support the regime, which in turn would support the university as we have come to know it. No, the American university nowadays has been reduced to an institution that simply *gets the job done,* whatever the job assigned to it might be, and by whomever assigned—federal bureaucrats, state legislators, feckless administrators, or politically tendentious faculty. The job of higher education, to the extent it plays any functional or aesthetic role with respect to our culture, is, in Wood's phrasing, to apply morticians' make-up to the corpse of Western civilization.

In chapter five, Susan E. Hanssen reminds us of a time, circa 1960, when "neo-scholastics and neo-classicists discovered, in retrospect, an idea of the American university to defend against the specialization and technocracy" that they thought might very well portend a new dark age. Men such as Christopher Dawson knew that they were eccentrics, peripheral to the fundamental drift of American history and the American university. What Dawson did not note, according to Hanssen, was that it was "precisely there—outside the center, outside the city, ostracized—that the greatest educators of his own tradition had found a very powerful magisterial chair." American civilization and Christian faith are in deep consonance with each other, but this consonance can be reinforced in the university only if the university itself retains its independence from the state.

Historically, American universities, in asserting their independence, were eccentric, but in this very eccentricity, decidedly *American.* Many gradually gave themselves over to the demands of specialization and technocracy that inevitably emanate from the center. But we have also seen eccentric resistance to this tendency and, in it, grounds for hope. As Hanssen points out, "The proliferation of independent schools and indeed the growing popularity of home-schooling is the most American feature in the panorama of education today; the continued attachment to classical liberal education and faith-based college curricula is the most distinctively American contribution to the varieties of higher education available today." Separation of emperor from pope—of state from church—is an idea at the core of Western civilization, and it is one that is perhaps best preserved in America. It points the way toward, and carves the space for, the preservation of the moral foundations of a civilization that are by their nature eccentric to the demands of the moment.

Part II of the book, which concentrates on the theme of higher education and democracy, is opened by William Mathie. We're all democrats now, and all proponents of liberal education, according to Mathie. And we tend to think that the two somehow mutually support each other. Yet true liberal education is an education in things that are alien to democracy. Socrates shows us the extent and nature of the disregard that the liberally educated must have toward the opinions of the many.

Yet Tocqueville points to the "naturalness" of democracy in contradistinction to its great antagonist, aristocracy—which is premised to a greater degree than democracy on fictions and illusions. If this is accurate, one might think democracy would provide the natural home for liberal education. But does a regime that overcomes a certain kind of illusion necessarily favor the pursuit of truth? Put another way, does democracy favor, or even provide the possibility conditions for, liberal education? Both Socrates and Tocqueville suggest not. In the exercise by democratic peoples of their right—and tendency—to judge for themselves, they inevitably fall back on the opinion of the majority, for there is no other source of intellectual authority in democratic ages. At least the *fiction* of superiority maintained by aristocracy allowed for the possibility of *actual* superiority.

Does then liberal education favor democracy? Tocqueville reminds us that the main guarantors of the American democratic republic are the mores—and especially religious mores—of her people, which are rather the opposite of the "liberal education" of her people. So, in either a Tocquevillian or Socratic framework, it seems that democracy does not support liberal education, and liberal education does not support democracy. What then can be the role—and idea—of the American university in its particular regime setting?

As Peter Lawler notes in the following chapter, individualist liberalism transforms all moral and communal certainties into questions. Therefore the heart and soul of the university—the professoriate—cannot be relied on to cultivate any of the virtues we might, from residual longing, associate with American higher education, whether these virtues be intellectual, spiritual, or civic. Professors once believed that students needed models of human greatness—models who would speak in their own words, but models who were to be put before the students *ab initio* by teachers who took their responsibilities seriously.

Nowadays, professors are more likely to believe, in Lawler's words, that "they're charged with liberating the students from 'the cave' or traditional or religious or bourgeois conformity to think for themselves. Yet, they must at least half-way know that their empty dogmas of non-conformism or self-creation or promiscuous libertarianism are a large part of the cave of any free and prosperous society." In light of this attempted liberation, the *liberal* part of liberal education continues to experience death by suicide. As Lawler mordantly reports: "Because of the emptiness of the autonomous alternative to productivity they promote, professors of humanities have just about put themselves out of business."

William B. Allen rounds out the consideration of higher education and democracy by noting that, as democrats, "we define higher education in the context in which almost everyone goes to college." The early twentieth century's goal of ensuring that all children graduated from high school has been extended to the university. This goal is linked to the purported immediate utility of higher education as an entrée into the working world. But Allen maintains that "Education really is about the development of the human soul to a level of proficiency that allows us to fulfill the promises of human potential." It is on this basis that we can begin to recapture the idea of the university, whose purpose must be to populate and repopulate the republic of letters. Elite universities fail miserably by this standard. Admitting the best while not demanding the best of them, they do nothing to augment the mind or soul of those who gain entrance.

Through open admissions, according to Allen, the university might aim at the loftier goal. Such a system would require the university to maintain the highest of standards, yet allow it to remain in consonance with progressive democratic aspirations. In other words, in demanding the best and not insulating students from failure, we see a means to recapture the idea of the American university that comports well with the regime in which the university operates.

The third and last part of the volume, on the university and the liberal arts, reminds us of a truth that educational reformers across the political spectrum often do not see: The "liberal arts" alone cannot ameliorate the crisis of the American university. Michael P. Foley begins by defining the liberal arts in Saint Augustine's terms, and contrasts them with the servile arts: "Simply put, while the servile arts were for gaining a livelihood, the liberal arts were for getting a life, for living life well." Yet Augustine was hardly unequivocal on the desirability of the liberal arts, for they are ambiguous with respect to the highest things that concern those who care about a life well lived. "The fecklessness of the liberal arts in the face of sin, their inability to liberate men and women from the worst kind of enslavement, is the central reason why he is loath to call them liberal."

Nor do these arts necessarily lead to the love of God, or to proper intellectual virtue, which depends on the mind's movement from the sensible but illusory world to the immaterial but real world. This grasping of the non-empirical occurs within an eminently Christian worldview. Nonetheless, the liberal arts can, according to Augustine, help us expose false thinking and help us understand the Bible and nature, and thereby at least prepare us for greater things. As Foley notes, "*if* the humanities were done with an eye towards the intelligible, they would be neither a self-absorbed bohemianism nor an ideological and capricious dismembering of a text or idea: they would be a study of the real, perhaps even of the more real." However, the university must also "foster both moral and religious excellence" in its students, "for without these great goods, a liberal education is as likely to become a poison as a remedy." As Foley allows, these are tall orders indeed for the contemporary American university. In the end, he suggests that the question we face is not whether Christianity can live with the liberal arts, but whether the liberal arts can live without Christianity.

John Agresto concludes the volume with further reflections on the subversive nature of what is passed off as liberal arts education today. He observes that the increasingly common understanding of the liberal arts "as *naturally* the opponents and critics of whatever society they occupy is so narrow, so diminished, and, in many cases, so self-destructive a view of the liberal arts that . . . the whole enterprise of liberal education cannot again prosper without its significant re-thinking." Far from liberating us from the drudgeries of existence or preparing us for what is beyond this world, the liberal arts are a central part of the new dogmatism of the American university. In Agresto's phrasing, "they cannot even talk any longer of 'thinking'—the rage is now 'critical thinking' . . . their aim is not to wonder, not to understand, not to explain but, simply, *to be critical.* The questioning of all orthodoxies and the destruction of all idols has become, today, the liberal arts' true work."

Such an understanding, perpetuated implicitly or explicitly by so many academic "proponents" of the liberal arts (and of philosophy in particular), is not so cleverly packaged as liberation, and sold to young adults whose souls are already glutted on this abundant and low hanging fruit of modernity. The understanding serves, of course, only to reinforce the very prejudices that so many 18 year olds bring to the university in the first place. And so the false embrace of Socrates, or, better, the embrace of a false Socrates, has led us away from the idea that all philosophy begins in wonder. And it leads us instead toward an institutionalized arrogance and superciliousness that passes as liberal learning.

So it is, Agresto suggests, that American higher education—and the souls of American students—are torn between philosophical nihilism, and modern science or business. And increasingly they gravitate toward the latter. In these disciplines, at least, the student is offered the only things that are alleged to be knowable—"just the facts, ma'am." And furthermore, mastery of these facts does seem—unlike the liberal arts—to ameliorate the human condition in concrete ways, not to mention offer the masters of the facts handsome livings for partaking in this amelioration.

So, we are left with important questions: Can the liberal arts be revived under such circumstances? But, perhaps more pressingly, should they be? America, after all, is not a land of aristocratic leisure, but of work, and productivity. So exactly what civic virtues, in the context of this regime, might the liberal arts inculcate, even if they were to be well taught, or even taught at all? Perhaps the inculcation of the higher virtues, including the civic ones, is best left outside the academy after all. And, as Agresto notes, those who would attempt a revival of the liberal arts must understand that if these arts no longer have suitors, it is because they are no longer lovely. And perhaps the same might be said of the American university itself.

I

The Life and Times of the American University

1

Universitas sine Universo

On the Home of Truth When There Is No Truth

James V. Schall, S.J.

We also see the individual ever more clearly fall into a state where he can be sacrificed without a second thought. The question thus arises whether we are witnessing the opening act of the spectacle to come, in which life appears as the will to power, and nothing else.

—Ernst Jünger, *On Pain*, 1934[1]

Everything evil is rooted in some good and everything false in some truth.

—Thomas Aquinas, I, 17, 4, ad 2

It may be remarked with equal truth that ignorance is often the effect of wonder. It is common for those who have never accustomed themselves to the labour of enquiry, nor invigorated their confidence by conquests over difficulty, to sleep in the gloomy quiescence of astonishment, without any effort to animate enquiry or to dispel obscurity.

—Samuel Johnson, *The Rambler*, no. 137, Tuesday, July 9, 1751

The Archbishop of Johannesburg, Buti Tlhagale, OMI, explained the intellectual structure of the late modern world to the South African Catholic Bishops' Conference in January of 2009. These are his words: "Post-modernity maintains that reality is a social construct, that truth is what you make of it. There is no objective truth. It further asserts that reality is a text to be interpreted and your interpretation is as valid as that of the next person. . . . Transcendence has become fictional. The individual has become the creator, free to shape his or her own destiny."

One wonders, of course, whether the "destiny" that we create for ourselves is the only one available, even granting our own supposed "self-creation." And we also wonder, when two "destines" are contradictory to each other, both of which we can freely concoct, how we can choose between them if there is no common world into which each must fit. I suppose that is the point. On that hypothesis, it does not make any difference what world we live in, nor does anything else. We live in the world we choose for ourselves. What else is there?

Classic realism means that a world exists and we know that it does. Human intelligence is oriented to the world as if to the purpose of both the world and the mind. *What is* stands as the standard or measure of what the mind knows. Truth means that the mind is conformed to a reality that it did not itself make, but nonetheless finds to be there.

In words, we express what is intelligible to the mind itself as well as intelligible to other beings with minds that hear. We do not create the world *that is*. We find it already there on discovering ourselves present within it. Neither do we create our minds or what it is to be mind. We act in this world according to what we are. We are rational beings that are free to do this or that. But we act only within the limits of our finite world where the things we find already in the world *are what they are*.

We are not, however, ultimately made for this world, though our path to our end passes through this world which is the scene and place of the drama that determines what we shall be through what we have been. This drama is why we are also political animals. We need this arena of human action while we live as mortals. My world and my neighbor's world are the same world even if we disagree with one another about what it is. Otherwise we could not argue about whose world is better. We did not cause ourselves to be or to be what we are. And we know that we did not.

We know ourselves only by knowing what is not ourselves. The gift that the world gives to each of us, apart from itself, is the conscious realization of ourselves, simultaneously with our seeking to know what is not ourselves. We know that we also exist as knowers. The principle of contradiction is affirmed implicitly in all we do, even in its denial. We cannot deny it without affirming it. This principle is the basis of being and thought about being. By being what it is, that is, something that cannot be otherwise than itself, the principle assures us that what we know in fact exists. The thing that we know in front of us cannot, at the same time, be something else. Hence, we can and do encounter real things, including rational beings who are not ourselves. With them, we can converse as if we are talking about something we all know or can know.

II

The Latin title affixed to this chapter is "*Universitas sine Universo.*" It is of my own concoction. Though it may seem otherwise, I do not intend this title to be esoteric. Indeed, I put it in Latin so that it would not be obscure.

Anyone can understand what these three words mean. Each is practically English anyhow, or better, the English came from the Latin. The first word means simply "university," the second means "without," and the third means "universe." The title is ironic. The notion that there is no common universe among us is, in itself, incoherent.

But philosophers can be found, or so they say, who would like it to be this way. If this "universe-less universe" were so, the university would not be related to or responsible to anything outside of itself, in particular to *what is*. To many, this situation already seems to be the academic situation. Modern universities do not study reality. They study themselves explaining the reality that is not there. The only judges they allow are other universities that do the same thing. Many have pointed out that the least diverse places in the modern world are universities, where, ironically, no common standard of judgment is acknowledged. Everything is alike in that its presumed difference makes no difference.

The other day, I saw a phrase in an announcement from the Catholic University of America. It contained a phrase from Nietzsche, or perhaps Fichte. It reads: "*Ex aliquo, nihil.*" This phrase, along with the title of this reflection, *Universitas sine Universo*, all play on the old principle, *Ex nihilo, nihil fit*—from nothing, nothing proceeds. Nor can something be created from nothing by that which is itself created. *Ex aliquo, sequitur aliquid.* It is from something that something else follows, but neither "something" explains why it is rather than is not.

The persistent fascination with *nihil*, with nothing, whether ancient or modern, I have always suspected, has something to do with a moral fear, not a metaphysical analysis. This moral fear intuits, whether it admits it or not, that something really exists. This being the case, an unsettling dread arises in our souls to the effect that *what is* exists as it does because it originates in the cause of *what is* in the first place. We cannot escape into nothing even in our own minds.

But we only "fear" this "cause of being" if we deny that "*Omne ens est bonum*," if we deny that evil, as such, must exist in a good being from which good can also still proceed. We instinctively see that the "Being" that is the source of the being in which each of us, as a *hoc aliquid*, participates, is itself *Ipsum Esse Subsistens*. It is the "I am who am" of Exodus. This latter is the only thing that can cause the being of all finite beings. And this finite being, so caused, is good. We too stand outside of nothingness. We know it as a fact about ourselves. We wonder why. And our wonder leads us to the certainty that we do not create ourselves. If we insist that we do make our own laws of being, we fear that we do have a judge of what we do with what we are. We are not, as Samuel Johnson said, "to sleep in the gloomy quiescence of astonishment without any effort to animate enquiry or to dispel obscurity."

III

The university is an institution deliberately set up in the middle ages for a definite purpose. It was a walled off enclosure where what is known in reason and what is known in revelation could address each other with no other reason than to find the truth of things. The university has the "being" of a corporation or of a relation, not that of a substance. Some universities were corporations of students that hired professors; others were of professors who invited students.

The university exists so that certain things can take place within its confines that do not easily occur outside of them. The modes of procedure were not the guns or rhetoric of politics, but the arguments of logic and intuition in the determination of truth. The university was neither designed as a home, nor a state, nor a Church, nor a world. It was a corporation, but not a business corporation. In principle, it only produced one thing, which was the truth of things in so far as the human mind could know it.

The words, *cosmos* and *universitas,* mean roughly the same thing. The first word, cosmos, however, means that all reality belongs together in a certain order of parts, distinguishable from one another yet for that reason related. The very purpose of the mind, as Robert Sokolowski affirmed, is to make these distinctions. We find this affirmation already in Plato. We are to say of *what is*, that it is, and of what is not, that it is not.

The second word, *universitas*, refers to an institution which exists for no other reason than the knowing of *what is*, than the knowing this order of the cosmos. This knowing includes the question of what we know about the where and why things are from whatever source. These things are examined, understood, affirmed, and made public. If we exclude from our *"universitas"* any source of knowledge that claims to be true we do not have a university.

The university was supposed to be limited by *what is*. It did not create reality but acknowledged it as already existing and therefore dependent on it. But it did assume that something intelligible was found in reality, including the human reality. When we read a novel, the plot, as a coherent whole, "exists," but not like you and I exist. It exists in the mind and words of its author, who, in his turn, exists as a human being. When the novel is studied in the university, its mode of existence is understood. The study of tales and novels does reveal something of reality, no doubt of it. This is why revelation is also proper to the purpose of a university. It too is mind directed to mind.

Indeed, in order for us live in this world, we need more than our own existence. We need to know how others have lived, what they have said and thought. We need history to come as close as we can to those who once did live the same mortal human life that we live, the same "four score years and ten," if we be given so long. We need the novel or the poem or the biography or the painting to come close to those who might have lived or who did live the existence that art gives the mind.

We can live more than our own minds in literature and in books of history. We suspect that somehow we are intended to know all of what is not ourselves. It is no accident that Aristotle defines the mind as that power we have that is *capax omnium*. Nor is it a total surprise that revelation, at bottom, is concerned with the resurrection of the body and eternal life, as if to say that none of our experiences are to be lost to any of us. We are not beings, ultimately, whose existence is "in vain."

IV

Of late, I have been interested in Stanley Fish's thesis about "The Last Professor." We might extrapolate, "What happens when the last professor disappears from the last university?" There is some considerable evidence that a university as such only existed in the western culture. In other words, its very existence requires certain understandings of reason and revelation that allow the dynamism of freedom and truth to work itself out. Or perhaps we can say that without the professor there is no university in the first place. The university is not a place of specialists, but a place of the whole that can only exist in a mind. This was the classical notion of wisdom.

Fish's concern is with the new informational brand of institution in which everything is broken up and specialized, in which no real concern with the real whole is any longer present. Aquinas, no doubt, taught us that if we are to understand things, we need to break the object down and work out a way step by step through to the whole. This is what his method of objections, articles, and answers to objections was about. In the Rambler from which I have been quoting, Samuel Johnson made the same point: "The chief art of learning, as Locke has observed, is to attempt but a little at a time. The widest excursions of the mind are made by short flights, frequently repeated." So it does seem that the place for specialization is the university.

Fish suspects that professors, in the classical sense, are dinosaurs. The professor was something more than a specialist. This is why the university, like a senate, was concerned with something more, with wisdom, with something that could not be acquired except after long reflection. It seems quite clear that students can matriculate in universities and learn nothing of what is important about God, cosmos, life, death, and what it all means.

Fish's question is whether wisdom has fled the university. Johnson put it this graphic way. "He that can only converse upon questions about which only a small part of mankind has knowledge sufficient to make them curious must lose his days in unsocial silence, and live in the crowd of life without a companion." A university should have professors who are wise in this sense. The student does not take his courses to learn about something, but about everything, about all that man throughout the years has learned. The danger of university life is the danger of intellectual life itself, the danger of pride.

Two of the most sobering things that I ever read about this danger implicit in the adventure of the intellectual life were found in Yves Simon's *A General Theory of Authority*. He wrote:

1. "No spontaneous operation of intellectual relations protects the young philosopher against the risk of delivering his soul to error by choosing his teachers infelicitously."[2]
2. "At philosophical conventions dead men make speeches for other dead men, and blind men play pantomimes for other blind men, and this will never prove anything against the intrinsic communicability of philosophic truth."[3]

How is it that we avoid the danger of choosing our professors "infelicitously" after I have just made the case that professors are in danger of disappearing from modern universities in favor of "instructors" and "specialists" who do not stay around long enough to discover wisdom? And further, where do we discover "philosophic truth" if the conventions of philosophers are inhabited by men who cannot hear or see the *things that are*?

V

I wish to conclude these remarks on a somewhat more personal note, but still in line of "the pursuit of truth when there is no truth" acknowledged. Perhaps it will clarify my title, "The University without a Universe." The university without a universe is a principle of relativism. I wish to reiterate what Eric Voegelin once said in a lecture, namely, that "Nobody needs to participate in the crisis of his time. He can do something else."[4] In order to "do something else," of course, one needs to know a) that there is a crisis and b) what else is there? In some sense, it is against this background that I have understood my own intellectual vocation, such as it is.

That you may understand what I am about, let me cite two instances that illustrate what I mean. But first, let me recall one of Isidore of Seville's maxims from the seventh century. He said: "A man must first be eager to understand what he is reading before he is fit to proclaim what he has learned." The eagerness cannot be had from the outside. One must have it from inside.

The first instance that I wish to recall is literary, the other is personal. I have often told others of both of these instances, but they are worth repeating. The first is found in Augustine's *Confessions*. I recount it to my new students every semester. If they understand the point being made, I think, they are on their way. They will have begun to know what it is to have a soul.

When Augustine was a young man, about nineteen or so, the age of the average college student, he was precocious, vain and worldly. But he was very smart, as all his friends knew. He wanted to be a teacher of rhetoric, which in Roman terms was the road to power. In today's terms, he wanted to be a lawyer. He was from a backwater place, Thagaste, in ancient Carthage, in modern day Tunisia.

Somehow, Augustine came across a now lost dialogue of Cicero, called the *Hortensius*. It was about philosophy. Augustine read this book. He was astonished by it. Then and there he put it down and decided that he wanted to be a philosopher himself. Imagine this scene of a nineteen year old Roman African reading a book of Cicero. This moment in an obscure place, with an utterly unknown young man in the hinterlands, reading a book, was of earth-shaking consequence for the rest of the world. Without that moment when Augustine decided to be a philosopher, there would have been no Augustine as we know him. Great things take place in obscurity.

The second instance that I wish to recall happened to me, also at nineteen. I was then in the Army stationed at Fort Belvoir, in Virginia, outside Washington. I had one semester of college at Santa Clara. World War II was over, the year was 1946. The draft was still on, but I signed up for an eighteen month enlistment, just to get it over with. But we really did not have much to do on base. On the Post, the usual USO library was found—nothing elaborate, but well-organized.

Knowing that I should read something, I recall going into the library one evening, looking at the stacks in the Dewey Decimal System. I suddenly realized, in a moment that has become ever clearer to me over the years, that I had no idea what to read. I had no "canon," no ordered guidance about what to read. What I do recall is that I did want to read something significant, whatever that was. This was a task I had largely been ignorant of in the previous nineteen years of my life.

What happened to me next was that I went back to Santa Clara and after a year joined the Society of Jesus. At that time, we were literally taken "out of the world," as they say, for about seventeen years, with not much to do but read. So I had time and occasion to make up for what I missed. But that experience of the Belvoir Post Library alerted me to the need people have of knowing what to read to get at the ultimate things. As the years passed, I found myself devising various lists and recommendations.

Those who know me well will probably be given the name of a book or two. You will also be told, "Read it." But my later teaching experience in Rome, San Francisco, and Washington, all mostly with nineteen year olds, made me realize that very few students really know what to read. Allan Bloom remarked that the unhappiest people in the modern world are those students in the twenty or thirty most expensive universities. If they are sharp, he thought, after experiencing what is there, they would realize that it is all unsatisfying and relative. So, as Lenin said, "What is to be done?"

VI

This year is the twentieth anniversary of the publication of a book of mine entitled *Another Sort of Learning*. Over the years, I have had many letters and e-mails about this book. Let me cite the book's rather elaborate sub-title, of which I am inordinately proud. But it approaches the response that I give to the issue of the modern professor and the modern multi-university, full of specialists, but, alas too often with little wisdom.

The sub-title reads as follows: "Selected Contrary Essays on How Finally to Acquire an Education While Still in College or Anywhere Else: Containing Some Belated Advice about How to Employ Your Leisure Time When Ultimate Questions Remain Perplexing in Spite of Your Highest Earned Academic Degree, Together with Sundry Book Lists Nowhere Else in Captivity to Be Found."

As I look at that title and sub-title now, together with other of my books in this genre, such as *Students' Guide to Liberal Learning*, *The Life of the Mind*, *On the Unseriousness of Human Affairs*, *The Order of Things*, and *The Sum Total of Human Happiness*, I realize that what I have been doing over the years was to provide students and adults, who came across such books, a way to acquire a learning that they likely were never given in their formal training in any college or university. This is why the phrase of the sub-title reads, "when ultimate questions remain perplexing in spite of your highest earned academic degree."

This sub-title was, in a sense, my effort to transcend the university and to give to students a way to be educated no matter what university they attended or how old they were. This is not in any way a "great books" program. I do not disdain great books, of course. But my approach is through what I call brief classics that no one will tell you about. Each book is short, incisive, exciting to read. Each book is about the truth.

Back in February, from out of nowhere, I received the following e-mail from a man, who tells me he is now forty, and about whom I know nothing. The letter is touching. I read it with a certain sense of unworthiness, but it makes the points that I want to leave you with, the point about Voegelin, about Augustine, about the Belvoir Post Library. The e-mail is addressed "Sir." It reads:

> I am waiting to board a flight and will be reading my well-loved copy of *Another Sort of Learning*. I wanted to thank you for writing it. It has been a gift in my life. When I was just out of high school, I was diagnosed with cancer. The treatment caused me to miss the normal college period of a young life. After all the surgeries and treatments, I ran for the mountains to wrestle with God. And He patiently wrestled back. In all of this I missed out on formal education. By the time I was ready I could not afford to attend. I was too busy earning my living. Your book opened up the exploration of not only why we are alive, but how to live well. It led to a better understanding of faith and life. For this I thank you.

Father Joseph Fessio, a good friend and the famed Director of Ignatius Press, which published *Another Sort of Learning*, once remarked that a book never knows who will read it. It is put out there and may or may not ever be seen again. An author does not know for whom he is writing. Chances are he won't know anyone who reads what he writes, or when it is read. It is like Augustine reading in some African hinterland a dialogue of Cicero, about four hundred years after it was written.

What I want to leave you with is this. Aquinas said that everything false is rooted in some truth. The question, Ernst Jünger wrote, is "Whether we are witnessing the opening act of a spectacle to come in which life appears as a will to power, and nothing else." We do not have to participate in the crises of our time. Universities rarely educate us in ultimate things. We have to find our way. We can still do this if, as I have tried to show over the years, we know what to read, and then read it.

What I learned in the library at Fort Belvoir is that we need some list lest we give our souls infelicitously to unworthy professors, either in the now or in the past. I have learned with Aquinas and, as Johnson said, even with Locke, that we need to break things down. But we also need to put them together again. This is what wisdom means, and our task in life is to become wise. Leo Strauss said that we are lucky if one or two of the greatest minds who have ever lived are alive in our time. Even if they are, we will be lucky to encounter them. But the main way we find them is in books, in what we read wisely.

Finally, one last word. Recently I was invited to give an invocation at a student sponsored banquet at Georgetown. Last year, I had given the main address to this same banquet. The young lady who ran the affair, whom I did not know and had not seen since last year, introduced herself. She said to me, "Last year you promised to give me a book list of what to read, but you never did." I am incapable of leaving such a challenge unmet. I went home and wrote her an email. I told her that I would list five very short books, those, as I like to say, to "keep sane by." The books were: 1) Leon Kass, *The Hungry Soul: Eating and the Perfection of Our Nature* 2) J. H. Bochenski, *Philosophy—an Introduction* 3) C. S. Lewis, *Till We Have Faces* 4) *Joseph Pieper—an Anthology* and 5) G. K. Chesterton, *Orthodoxy*. I finished by adding one book of my own, namely, *On the Unseriousness of Human Affairs*. In case you wonder, I never heard whether she went ahead and read any of these incisive books.

So with these books, I will leave you. I think that you will find these and the others indicated in *Another Sort of Learning* to touch the "ultimate things" that nobody told you about while you were in college. Ultimately, what you want and look for is a wise professor, for someone who will tell you the truth of things. What is up to you is your soul—whether you will listen and whether you will, with Plato, say of *what is* that it is, and of what is not, that it is not. Whether, with Isidore, you will to be eager to learn and to know.

There is a university even if there is no "universe." This university exists in books no one will tell you about. When you read them, you will discover the universe, the cosmos, and you will be delighted. We are not to "sleep in a gloomy quiescence of astonishment" unwilling to make "any effort to animate enquiry or dispel obscurity." Everything false is "rooted in some truth." We do not "create ourselves." We already are more than we could ever imagine. *Sapientis est ordinare.* It is the function of the wise man to know the order of things. We are not to spend our days in "unsocial silence." It is not our purpose when we seek an education to know something. It is our function to know everything, to know *all that is.*

NOTES

1. Ernst Jünger, *On Pain*, translated with an Introduction by David C. Durst, with a Preface by Russell A. Berman (New York: Telos Press, [1934] 2008), 45.

2. Yves Simon, *A General Theory of Authority* (Notre Dame: University of Notre Dame Press, 1980), 100.

3. Simon, *A General Theory of Authority*, 112.

4. *Conversations with Eric Voegelin* (Montreal: Thomas More Institute, 1980), 33.

2

The End of the American
Core Curriculum

Mark C. Henrie

Ever since the 1980s, American conservatives have advanced a spirited critique of the American university. Landmark books by Allan Bloom (*The Closing of the American Mind*, 1987), Roger Kimball (*Tenured Radicals*, 1990), and Dinesh D'Souza (*Illiberal Education*, 1991) shaped the contours of a compelling narrative that has become conventional: Relativism, the fruit of insidious postmodern high theory imported from Europe, has poisoned the humanities; courses and entire disciplines have been politicized along race, class, and gender lines by a generation of tenured radicals; diversity has displaced academic merit as the academy's key value; young minds are no longer opened by a lively encounter with the best that has been thought and said, but rather, they are subjected to an intellectually deadening indoctrination into multicultural orthodoxies. It is a harrowing bill of indictment, and the fact that books advancing such theses quickly won a wide readership indicates that they captured a genuine truth in want of articulation.

In the now standard conservative narrative, "the Sixties" stand as a watershed separating the dismal present from halcyon days of yore. In Allan Bloom's classic retelling, the turning point came when antinomian student upheavals were met with sheepish acquiescence on the part of a spineless liberal professoriate. Up to that point, it would seem, all was well with the American university. If Allan Bloom was a reactionary—a charge frequently leveled—the *status quo ante* he sought to restore was not some impossibly distant prospect. Rather, it was merely something like the University of Chicago of Bloom's youth in the 1950s. The same is true of the great majority of mainstream conservative criticisms of the contemporary university. Upon consideration, their aims are actually quite modest. They seek a "non-politicized" form of higher education, which they take to be "traditional" in modern America before the 1960s. Very rarely do conservative critics offer a substantive alternative to the basic structures of the modern university.

But what exactly *was* the "traditional" form of the modern American university from which we have tumbled headlong since the Sixties? Was it adequate, even for its time? Is it, in fact, desirable to return to it today? Or are more radical curricular reforms needed? These are intricate questions. To approach them, we will assay the real changes that have occurred to university curricula since the 1960s. As we will see, the heart of the matter lies—as well it might—with the Core Curriculum.

I

By the middle of the twentieth century, American university curricula displayed a certain balanced understanding of their educational mission, representing a prudent spirit of adaptation in light of new educational emphases. Room was made for new elements, but there was reluctance to eliminate older forms. The result was a rather healthy eclecticism in course requirements. Various dimensions of intellectual virtue were each given their due: the basic cultural knowledge by which an educated man situates himself in the world and in history; a broad exposure to various methods of inquiry; the mastery and intellectual command that are the fruit of disciplinary specialization. Programmatically, this balance was achieved by a Core Curriculum in the literary, philosophical, and artistic monuments of Western civilization; a diverse set of requirements in General Education; and a carefully structured course of studies in a major. How are these elements faring today, four decades on from the transformations begun in the Sixties?

The Major

The system of majors still flourishes, and to a large degree the self-governing disciplines have by now become the dominant feature of the university. In the 1950s, it was at least imaginable that an inspiring teacher, devoted to his institution and well liked by his colleagues, might achieve tenure despite a spotty record of research and publishing; such an outcome is no longer imaginable. The strength of the disciplines reflects the still high prestige of the natural sciences on which they are modeled. This strength reflects, as well, the guild-like structure of the Ph.D. system which credentials faculty and serves as the basis for their institutional authority. Yet outside the natural sciences, the structured sequencing of courses within the major, one course building upon another and probing to a deeper level, has been largely abandoned. Professors today are more committed to their own research than to their teaching obligations, and so they resist a "rigid" curricular plan that would require them to prepare courses in unfamiliar topics for the sake of curricular coherence. Moreover, faculty members themselves have fundamental disagreements about the nature of their disciplines and so find it impossible to reach a consensus about the "end" toward which a course of studies should be directed. The faculty's solution has been to avoid direction.

Students in a major are thus largely free to pick and choose as they please, and as the current course offerings allow. Consequently, many students experience their major in a rather aimless way: the major does not "progress" or "culminate" in the sense of *command* which is its reason for being. Graduating students often do not understand themselves to have achieved even preliminary mastery of a subject area. Whereas "critical" methods of teaching and learning have been "pushed forward" to earlier and earlier years of study in the past generation—even middle schoolers are now taught "critical thinking," whatever that is—mastery of a discipline (in fields outside the natural sciences) has usually been "pushed back" to the M.A. years of graduate school.

Responding to this charge of aimlessness, from time to time university administrations have sought in recent years to strengthen the major by instituting a required "culminating experience," either a thesis or a long research paper. In such an approach, however, the undergraduate major is understood to have as its *end* primarily the production of future graduate students in the discipline—the "culminating experience" mimics what would be expected of a Master's student. It is as if the only goal of the undergraduate study of, for example, economics, is to become a professor of economics (rather than a businessman, banker, lawyer, etc.). The very strength of the disciplines *as disciplines* therefore raises questions about the educational program of the university as a whole.

General Education and Distributive Requirements

A system of distributive and other general education requirements has also continued to flourish since the Sixties. Commonly, students will find that they are required to reach a certain low-level proficiency in a foreign language, they will need to demonstrate command of written English, and they will be required to take a prescribed number of courses in a range of fields of study.

The theoretical justification for requirements in general education is *broad* exposure to various bodies of knowledge and approaches to understanding. There is an echo here of John Henry Newman's argument that a university is "a place of teaching universal knowledge," and that failure to take the measure of all areas of inquiry results in a kind of deformity of the intellect. Some students may grumble at these requirements, which take them away from pursuing their major subject with single-mindedness, and frequently faculty members sympathize with such complaints. After all, the professors have themselves undertaken graduate studies in increasingly narrow fields; their liberal education is many years in the past, and their self-esteem depends on their standing in their particular disciplines, not on their reputation for the synthetic skills of the generalist. But Newman's argument about the humane value of broad learning remains compelling.

There is also a simply practical advantage to distributive requirements. Today, about two-thirds of all students will change their major during their college career and many will change more than once. What students will "be" in life is almost certainly not what they thought they would "be" when they set off for college. Distributive requirements offer an opportunity to view the world from different intellectual perspectives. Who knows but that an unexpected horizon may prove to correspond to the heart's deepest longings?

The Core Curriculum

So two key dimensions of the balanced educational program of the "traditional" American university have survived and even thrived since the watershed of the Sixties. It is the core curriculum—a survey of the great works of Western civilization—which has fared the worst in the curricular reforms of the past generation. With few exceptions, the core curriculum has been simply *eliminated* from American higher education. When all is said and done, the demise of the core curriculum is *the* major structural change that separates the curriculum of the 1950s from the curriculum of today.

Those of a suspecting cast of mind may speculate that this change has occurred for reasons having to do with vested interests. Following the model of the natural sciences, Ph.D.s in the humanities are rewarded for original "contributions to knowledge." But the great works of Western culture have been studied for centuries. What genuinely "new" insights can be gleaned there? Have aspiring humanities Ph.D.s perhaps turned, in desperation, to other subjects where there is still something new to be said? If so, how can they be expected to teach the great books, which were not their subject of study?

The elimination of the core is also surely the result of a moral rejection: The generation of the Sixties, which admired the Viet Cong and cheered U.S. defeat in Southeast Asia, viewed their own civilizational heritage as a legacy not to be honored but to be overcome. The "privileging" of the great works of the West therefore had to end.

A more positive justification for the demise of the core is frequently given, however. In order to prepare students for the Multicultural World of Tomorrow, it is said, students must be exposed to the *diversity* of world cultures. A merely Western curriculum would be parochial, a failure of liberal learning, which is properly universal in its scope. Moreover, since our modern or postmodern technological civilization is characterized by rapid change, it is more important to be exposed to "approaches to knowledge," to "learn how to learn," than it is to acquire any particular body of knowledge. But education then becomes nothing but the cultivation of abstract instrumental rationality, divorced from any content and divorced from any end. Consistent with these arguments, many universities now call their *distributive requirements* a "core curriculum." They claim to have undergone curricular development rather than curricular demise.

As a practical matter, this multicultural transformation of the curriculum can have two curious results. In the worst cases, what passes for a multicultural "core curriculum" is nothing but a peculiar kind of Western echo chamber. Students are given over to studying Marxist critics in contemporary Algeria and neo-Marxist critics in contemporary Brazil and post-Marxist critics in contemporary France. All that is really learned are variations on the "critique of ideologies"—a powerful legacy of one great Western mind, that of Karl Marx. In other cases, however, students really are exposed to the high cultures and great works of non-Western societies: They are invited to savor, for example, the works and deeds of Suleiman the Magnificent or the humane subtleties of the Chinese sage Mencius; but their encounter with *Western* high culture remains slight, and when they do encounter our tradition, they are invited not to savor it, but to deconstruct it. We thus are presented with the spectacle of many students today who habitually associate high ideals, penetrating insight, and profound wisdom with just about every culture but their own.

II

To assess the significance of the late-twentieth-century demise of the American core curriculum, it is important to understand from whence the mid-twentieth-century core came and what it was *not.* I say "what it was *not*" because we too often concentrate on the continuity of the enterprise of higher learning, when in fact the differences over the centuries are equally worthy of reflection. The very term "core" curriculum implies that these studies lie at the heart of the mission of a university. But when it comes to articulating the essence of liberal learning, the university's—and hence, a core curriculum's—end or *telos*, we tend to fall into high-minded rhetoric that appeals to our magnanimity but obscures key distinctions.

For example, Allan Bloom's famous book is taken by most to constitute a flamboyantly brilliant restatement of a "traditional" defense of a "traditional" curriculum. And certainly, much of the rhetoric of *The Closing of the American Mind* trades on tropes from Matthew Arnold and John Henry Newman. But it takes little effort to see that there are quite distinctive features to Bloom's account of the excellences of an education centered on Great Books. He insists that such books must be approached ahistorically. He emphatically denies that the traditional Western canon ought to be read because it is in any sense "our own." He seldom speaks of truth, and *delectio in veritate*, delighting in the truth—which Augustine held to be the end of inquiry—appears to be beyond his ken. Instead, he seduces his readers with voluptuous hints at the intellectual pleasures of penetrating to unsettling philosophical depths. There is very little that is "traditional" in any of this, and in fact, the stupendous success of Bloom's book has perhaps done more than anything else to obscure a more genuinely traditional defense of the Western canon in our time.

Whence, then, came the American core of the mid-twentieth century, and what were its peculiar features? What were the intellectual values its served? What was its *telos*? Medieval universities were famously Scholastic: They aimed to convey mastery of a *science*, whether divinity, philosophy, medicine, or law. In effect, they were at their core professional schools, teaching technical bodies of knowledge not from primary texts but from digests and textbooks such as the *Sentences* of Peter Lombard. A characteristic exercise was the *disputation*—learned debate on advanced questions in a field. Ideas of "broad" learning such as we find in Newman had no place in the medieval curriculum. We would likely not be able to recognize this higher education as either "liberal" or "humane." We might even say that it was an early instance of the power of *Wissenschaft*. Certainly the writings of Abelard display not a sense of wonder, or of humanistic largeness of soul, but rather a sense of the intellectual *power* that command of dialectical method places in the hands of an adept.

During the Renaissance, the sophisticated speculative logic-chopping which had been the glory of Scholasticism was effectively denigrated by a new humanism which prized instead erudition in the primary texts of classical Greek and Roman authors and rhetorically stylish expression of thought. The exhaustive treatise gives way, at length, to the essay. From the perspective of a Scholastic master, the Renaissance man appears to be a species of dilettante. From the perspective of the Renaissance man, the Scholastic master appears to labor, hidebound, over matters of no great importance. What is curious about this historical turn is that it is an instance in which *rhetoric* is judged to possess a dignity higher than that of *dialectic*—for the Scholastics surely excelled at demonstrative arguments, whereas the humanists engaged in satire, diatribe, and other less-than-demonstrative rhetorical appeals. For those of us who have been influenced by the Platonic tradition, there is something unnatural about "mere rhetoric" winning the day against dialectic. Yet this is what happened. This strange inversion was made possible only because in medieval times dialectic had focused so single-mindedly on God as its subject. As the name "humanist" suggests, the turn at this juncture is in the direction of *human* wisdom, where the certainty of demonstrative argument is naturally less available; the gaze of the mind's eye was averted from the divine realities that had been the Scholastics' theme. The humanities moved to the center of the university, displacing divinity.

From about the end of the sixteenth century up through the middle of the nineteenth, there was remarkable stability to university curricula in the West. The classics were studied, in their original languages (especially Latin—many Greek works were read in Latin translation), because of a general cultural consensus that the ancients were *better* than us—and so, to be emulated. To be an educated man was to have facility with Latin and a classicizing imagination—the ability to see in the ancients the visage of revered elder brothers. Thus, circa 1850, throughout most of the West and including America, the study of modern writers such as Montesquieu or Rousseau would *not* have constituted part of a university's required core offerings. Nor, for that matter, would the study of Thomas Aquinas or Cajetan have been a requirement in Catholic universities. All these would have been specialized studies to be undertaken by advanced scholars with a particular interest, not by undergraduates in their required curriculum. The common core remained, for an astonishing stretch of time—more than three hundred years—the writings of Greece and Rome, and little else. To possess a baccalaureate meant that one knew the Classics.

America's universities began in this milieu, and they participated fully in this classical model. Indeed, at least one critic has come to the judgment that it was because of American colleges' devotion to classicism that those institutions were of no intellectual or practical importance before the Civil War—all that really mattered in America then was "happening" elsewhere. However, American universities were, from the beginning, somewhat different from their European counterparts. For one thing, they were born in a non-aristocratic society, and so the classical model—so obviously attractive to aristocratic Europe—was subject to constant critique (though usually from outside the university, and usually ineffectually). For another, they were decidedly post-Reformation foundations, with only few exceptions denominational colleges, and so Biblical religion played a relatively larger role than in Europe—though it was a religion shorn of pre-Reformation theological traditions.

American universities modernized—or, one might say, Germanized—quite rapidly after the Civil War, introducing the complete model of *Wissenschaft*, with graduate studies, the Ph.D., the system of majors and electives, and an emphasis on the natural sciences. It was a true revolution in pedagogy. By the earliest years of the twentieth century, even backward colleges such as Dartmouth had jettisoned Greek and Latin entrance requirements. In England, this transformation would happen later, and it would never be quite complete until very recently. In Germany, this transformation had already occurred earlier in the nineteenth century—but there, the *Gymnasia* nevertheless retained their profoundly classical orientation up until the Second World War. This was not the case in the United States, where modernization of the university went hand-in-hand with a Deweyite modernization of the high schools. One might say that by the First World War, America had out-Germanized the Germans in achieving an educational system dominated by scientific pursuits organized by disciplines.

It was in this context, in the first half of the twentieth century, that what we recognize as the "traditional" American core curriculum was born, in the context of galloping instrumental rationality in the form of German *Wissenschaft*. Leading American universities began to re-introduce required course sequences exploring and explaining the history of the West, with generous use of great texts. (That this restorative movement did not occur in the high schools as might be thought more natural—aping the still-classical German *Gymnasium*—is a peculiarity of the American experience that requires an explanation.)

It might be said that the core curriculum was a "political" solution to a "political" problem within the university: What to do with all those (seemingly useless) classicists and other humanists? Thinking up the core curriculum was a work of inspired deanship, perhaps. But it was more than that. It was also a response to the realization that something had been lost in modernization, that *Wissenschaft* alone did not suffice, that man does not live by technical expertise alone. There is something *human* that does not admit to study through "scientific" methods but which must be approached . . . humanistically, through human beings' characteristic creation, culture.

The core curriculum was a political solution in another sense, however. Columbia's "Contemporary Civilization" seminar was a response to the First World War. Harvard's General Education was a response to the Second World War and the incipient Cold War. One of the compelling rationales for the core curriculum was therefore to justify "what we are fighting for." As a result, the history of the West was almost always presented in Whig terms—with noble progressives fighting to achieve advances against backward-looking conservatives. On the whole, the American core culminated in a vindication of the American Way of Life—capital A, capital W, and capital L. As the so-called "Allied Scheme of History" sought common political and cultural ground among the British, the French, and the Americans, over against "the Hun"—the Germans—there was also a tendency to see in nineteenth-century German thought an antithesis of the "true" West which was perhaps without warrant.

The American core curriculum that emerged differs from the classical curriculum of the sixteenth through the nineteenth centuries. For one thing, the works treated in the courses were taught in translation, since the classical languages were no longer the common possession of educated men and women. What is more, the courses were not predicated on the superiority of Greece and Rome; the civilization of antiquity was, instead, understood as a forerunner to modernity's greater achievements. While the core aspired to cover the entire 2,500-year history of "the West," reflecting its American provenance, great emphasis was placed on the early-modern sources of the American regime. Reflecting the crisis of the early twentieth century, special emphasis was also placed on nefarious nineteenth-century German thinkers. In effect, for Americans, early-modernity became "our antiquity," the moment of privileged synthesis which led to the founding of the "New Rome" that is the United States.

The objection of the multicultural Left to such a curriculum is that it privileges one particular culture, our own, over others. This, it is said, is a form of pedagogic injustice. Such an education is not truly "liberal" or "universal" but is, instead, a form of ethnocentric indoctrination. That the American core curriculum emerged in the context of the world wars lends some credence to this charge. It is insufficiently acknowledged, however, that the recent conservative defenders of the core such as Bloom usually themselves stipulate that education as Western enculturation would, indeed, be indoctrination. They have no interest in defending the core in such terms. Indeed, Bloom and his followers avoid the very word *culture*—for culture is not a natural substance. Particular cultures change in time and so have no eternal essence. In a strictly Platonic reckoning, cultures cannot be objects of philosophical questioning. There's no "there" there. The question of culture is not the Platonic "What is . . . ?" but rather "Who are we?" And that is a question that can only be answered provisionally, historically—i.e., less than philosophically. Bloom therefore turns to the Great Books only as an appropriately privileged *occasion* for an opening to genuine philosophical inquiry. It is such opening, and such inquiry—and those alone—that are truly "liberal" and "universal."

The Left's charge of indoctrination in the traditional American core curriculum cannot be dispatched as easily as one might wish. And Bloom's argument is powerful, and conveyed with a seductive highmindedness that is difficult to resist. Who is there who would not like to boast of having achieved true philosophy rather than mere erudition in one's own tradition? But is the argument that education as enculturation amounts to nothing more than indoctrination finally compelling? Is there really *no* educational or intellectual value in examining one's cultural history *because it is one's own*? After all, while the question, "Who are we?" may not admit of philosophical exactitude, it is nevertheless a very *human* question, and an urgent one.

There are really two arguments for the traditional core; properly speaking, the core has two ends in view. They concern the importance of high culture and the importance of history.

High Culture

In recent years, a not uncommon sight on a university campus during freshman week has been a group of students sitting on the grass in the evening, one with a guitar, singing together the theme songs of vintage television sitcoms. In a society as diverse as America at the dawn of the twenty-first century, this is to be expected: Television is one of the few things which young people from all walks of life have in common. But what are we to think when the same scene is repeated in senior week, four years later? Has higher education done its job when the only common references of those with a baccalaureate degree remain those of merely popular culture?

The core curriculum is the place in university studies where one encounters what Matthew Arnold called "the best that has been thought and said"—and does so because it is the best. Such a view of education is hierarchical, discriminating, judgmental. It reflects the fact that the high can be distinguished from the low, and the further understanding that the high can comprehend the low whereas the low can never take the measure of the high. By spending time with the best, with the highest expressions and reflections of a culture, the mind of the student is equipped for its own ascent. Without such an effort, the student remains trapped in the unreflective everyday presumptions of the current culture: the student remains trapped in clichés. The high culture of the traditional core curriculum is therefore *liberating*, as befits the liberal arts.

Throughout history there have been countless thinkers, poets, writers, and artists; the vast majority of all their labor has been lost, and most of them have been entirely forgotten. What survives are the truly great works which have been held in consistent high esteem through the changing circumstances of time and place. Thus, the traditional canon of great books—the common possession of educated men and women across the centuries—is not an arbitrary list, nor does the canon reflect relations of "power"; rather, as Louise Cowan has observed, the classics of a civilization "select themselves" by virtue of their superior insight. The presumptions and presuppositions of our lives, which lie so deep in us that we can scarcely recognize them, are in the great works made available for inspection and inquiry. High culture is a matter not of snobbish refinement but of superior (self-) understanding.

It is here that the core curriculum is indispensable. For every student brings to college a *preliminary* "enculturation"—we have all by the age of eighteen absorbed certain perspectives, insights, narratives, stereotypes, and values that communicate themselves to us in the prevailing popular culture. This enculturation is a common possession of a generation, typically spanning the diversity of family backgrounds, class, and ethnicity. But the artifacts of *popular* culture are always mere reflections of the possibilities glimpsed and made possible by works of high culture. The traditional core curriculum provides a student with access to that high culture; its *higher* "enculturation" provides a student with a vantage point from which he can grasp the meaning and implications of his everyday cultural presumptions. He begins to hold something in common with the educated men and women of past ages; they become his peers. And he possesses as a result a standpoint from which genuinely critical reflection becomes possible.

One of the peculiar presumptions of our time is that of novelty. Social and technological transformations have given us a prejudice against tradition and in favor of "originality." But it is the great works of the traditional canon which constitute the record of true originality: That is why they have survived. Only by becoming familiar with them are we enabled to recognize just how derivative is much of that which now passes as original insight and invention. A university that does not orient students to high culture effectively commits itself to a project of deculturation, and thereby traps its students in a kind of permanent adolescence. A core curriculum therefore aims at a form of human maturity. It invites a student to put away childish things.

History

George Santayana famously asserted that those who do not remember the past are condemned to repeat it, and Cicero centuries earlier observed that to know nothing of the world before one's birth is to remain always a child. These cautionary aphorisms are perfectly and pointedly true, and in the first instance they constitute one justification for the historical studies undertaken in a core curriculum. Practically speaking, there is wisdom to be found in experience. This wisdom is never more fully appreciated than when we experience the consequences of our actions at first-hand. But because human affairs exhibit certain recurring patterns, knowledge of history provides a stock of experiences at second-hand from which more general "lessons" may be drawn as well—at least, by those with ears to hear and eyes to see.

Nevertheless, these admonitions of Santayana and Cicero do *not* constitute the truly decisive historical reason for embarking on the traditional core curriculum. After all, insofar as human affairs exhibit patterns, and insofar as we approach history merely in search of the generally applicable "laws" or "rules" of human interaction, one may as well find one's stock of lessons in any given civilization as in any other. If history is merely an undifferentiated field of repeating examples of the universal nature of human societies, then anyone's history is as good as anyone else's. It is because the contemporary academic mind views the matter in just this social-scientific way that it is necessarily driven to understanding the traditional core curriculum's Western focus as nothing but the result of chauvinism or laziness.

But the core curriculum's particular emphasis on Western history is not the result either of ethnocentrism or of sloth. There is something far deeper going on here. Indeed, when history is approached merely as the raw material of social science, historical study in itself loses any *intrinsic* value; all that really matters in such a scheme are the "laws" which are abstracted from the pool of historical "examples." The core curriculum, however, does mean to value history *in itself.* How so?

All of us are born into a natural world governed by laws not of our making. Some of these laws are the laws of human nature and of human interaction, laws that apply in every time and place. But all of us are also born into the historical world at a particular time, and there is a certain *unrepeatable* (and unpredictable) quality to each historical moment, the result of free human choices. What is more, the historical moment we inhabit *now* is the outcome, in part, of the contingent history of our particular community, both recently and more remotely. In order to answer the first question of every true inquirer—*What is going on here?!*—it is necessary to uncover the historical narrative of the present: That is, it is necessary to answer the question, What is going on *now*? To answer this question in any profound sense, it is necessary to understand the historical narrative of one's own civilization—to understand, as well, what was going on *then*. Consequently, the traditional core curriculum is *not* simply the study of the great books of the Western world isolated from their historical contexts; rather, that study proceeds side-by-side with an inquiry that locates those works in history. While the great works articulate the great human possibilities, not all human possibilities are equally available to us today, nor equally available everywhere. In effect, to understand the meaning of that relative availability (and unavailability) is to understand one's place in history.

Typically, when a core curriculum has been poorly constructed, it reads history in a Whiggish way, "progressively." Western history tells the simple tale of how the world has progressed ever upward until it reaches its high-point, the present (and in particular, *me*). Moreover, such a facile historical sense anticipates a future that is a straight-line extrapolation of the present. When the core is structured well, however, it leaves open the question of whether the present is the outcome of progress or decline. (The truth, it has been said, is that things are always getting both better and worse, at the same time.) A student who has learned the deep historical lessons of a core cur-riculum is also just as alert to the possibilities of historical transformation just ahead—the possibilities of *metanoia*, or conversion—as he is to the possibil-ity of continuity.

III

The worthy goals of the traditional American core curriculum, then, were intellectual elevation and orientation. The core aimed to raise one's sights, and also to locate cultural and historical—that is to say, human—landmarks, both near at hand and on the far horizon, by which to reckon. Whether or not such a core led to the ecstatic philosophy held out by Allan Bloom, it surely fostered a kind of intellectual *maturity*, the ability to place things, and oneself, in perspective—the ability to connect the present concerns of the self with a larger and deeper narrative. Is it too much to say that the core uniquely served the Delphic injunctions, "Know thyself" and "Nothing too much"? That, at least, was the ideal.

The actual core curricula that flourished in the middle decades of the twentieth century were, of course, not perfect. In their accounts of the West, they tended to dwell on the Greeks to the serious neglect of the Romans; they could discern nearly nothing of importance in the Middle Ages; they conflated theology with Biblical criticism on the one hand and poetry (Dante, Milton) on the other. In these respects, those curricula bore the marks of Enlighten-ment and Romanticism: They betrayed their twentieth-century American provenance. To say that actual core curricula were not all they could be is, however, no fatal objection to the project. Reform and improvement might have been called for, but not abolition.

The purpose of the core was in any event *not* to inculcate any kind of Western chauvinism—certainly not any ethnocentrism that would prevent a student from exploring and learning from non-Western cultures. If anything, the old core may be said to have approached the evident superiority of the modern West as a puzzle in need of solving—hence the pains taken to understand the West's history; for all the multicultural pieties of today's university, the implicit presumption of the universality of contemporary civilization forecloses serious questioning either of the Self or of the Other. Be that as it may, one suspects that it is precisely those who have delved most thoughtfully into the wisdom of the Occident who are in a position to learn the most from the wisdom of the Orient—rather like Matteo Ricci and the other Jesuits who encountered Chinese civilization with such sympathetic results in the seventeenth century. Lacking a foundation in the depths of our own civilization, a student can approach another civilization as little more than a tourist.

And indeed, is that not a fit description of even elite college students in our time? With the internet as their facile guidebook, they are naively self-assured technocratic tourists, carting about in their intellectual backpacks all the fashionable certainties of the age, together with an oddball collection of facts and theories picked up haphazard along their educational way. They are as bright as ever students have been, and some will of course become quite advanced in a particular discipline. But they have not been prepared to sustain in common an intellectual culture of any depth—the very possibility of doing so has never been presented to them—and they are utterly naïve about the historicity of the present age.

In the years when the core curriculum flourished in the American academy, figures such as Karl Barth and Reinhold Niebuhr appeared on the cover of *TIME* Magazine. It was taken for granted that a college-educated general readership would want to keep abreast of serious intellectual developments in a range of fields. A great debate raged in the quarterlies, worrying over the emergence of so-called "middlebrow culture": A bastardized declension from truly high culture. In our own time, *Wikipedia* places the world at students' fingertips—and it offers entries on comic book superheroes that are lengthier and more detailed than those on Karl Barth or Reinhold Niebuhr. And in an age when professors write (admittedly ingenious) books on *Buffy the Vampire Slayer*, "middlebrow" seems a brow too far.

The excision of the core curriculum was to have signaled the arrival of an ideal cosmopolitan culture of higher learning in the American university. Instead, students have never been more trapped in the parochial clichés of the present age.

3

From Civilizational Memory and the Upward Lifting of Souls, to Upward Mobility, to Upending Social Mores

The Going Down of University Education in One Professor's Lifetime

Gary D. Glenn

Tocqueville's America had little place for what he once called "higher education."[1] One reason is that "in democracies individual interest and those of the state demand that education for most people should be scientific, commercial and industrial rather than literary."[2] American circumstances "fix the mind of the American on purely practical objects."[3] Even in the arts, democratic people "encourage a taste for the useful more than the love of beauty."[4] Democracies "think about nothing but ways of changing their lot and bettering it . . . every new way of getting wealth more quickly, every machine which lessens work, every means of diminishing the costs of production, every invention which makes pleasures easier or greater, seems the most magnificent accomplishment of the human mind. It is chiefly from this line of approach that democratic people come to study sciences, to understand them, and to value them. In aristocratic ages the chief function of science is to give pleasure to the mind, but in democratic ages to the body."[5]

He writes an entire chapter on "Why the Americans are more concerned with the applications than with the theory of science."[6] The gist is that a democratic way of life leaves either little opportunity or taste for "meditation" and hence "the darting speed of a quick, superficial mind is at a premium, while slow deep thought is excessively undervalued."[7]

If Tocqueville is right, then one should expect American universities to provide an emphatically practical and useful education in service of the pleasures of the body and not of the cultivation of the mind. The first purpose of this paper is to show that universities have done just that. The second purpose is to trace the steps in the going down of the "higher" education of the mind and soul. The third purpose is to try to identify the causes and circumstances which brought American universities into closer congruence with democratic society as Tocqueville understood it. In what follows, I will reflect on these purposes through my personal experiences, accumulated over the 50 years I have spent in universities.

UPLIFTING THE SOUL

In February 2008, about 100 feet from my first floor university office, five students were murdered during a class. A former student walked into the class and opened fire with at least two guns, killing them and himself. The police were never able to unearth either a clear motive or evidence that those close to him had intimations of his impending action.

In subsequent days, two photos of the murderer were published that were suggestive and revealing of the state of his soul. In one, he was wearing a t-shirt on the back of which is a quote from Nietzsche: "He who fights with monsters might take care lest he thereby become a monster. And if you gaze for long into an abyss, the abyss gazes also into you."[8]

The second photo focused on his arms. The Associated Press described what the photo showed: "his arms [were] blanketed with disturbing tattoos, including a skull pierced by a knife, a pentagram and a macabre character from the 'Saw' horror movies, superimposed on images of bleeding slashes across his forearm."[9] One might impartially characterize this description as redolent of having looked "for long" into the abyss so that the abyss, by gazing back into his soul, had imprinted itself there.

The point is not that reading Nietzsche led to the murders. Rather, I have found no published commentary which stated or implied that the universities he attended had, or should have had, anything to do with uplifting his soul so that it would be appalled by, rather than attracted to, looking into that abyss. Indeed, in the published commentaries, I did not find the word "soul" at all. There was talk instead of "mental illness," but in such a way that *nothing* was attributed, however speculatively, to what he had studied, or not studied, in the university. In particular, in light of Tocqueville's comment above, no one suggested that the university should have tried to teach him repugnance of the hideous and ugly with which he had covered his arms by trying to teach him to love beauty.

I take it that this finding surprises no one who knows that forming the soul to love the good and the beautiful is no longer an expected part of education in modern American universities. While one may still discuss and teach "ethics," the idea of forming souls has largely disappeared. Where it still exists in universities, it is essentially a private interest about which some faculty and students might somehow care.

An experience from last summer might be evidence that even the word "soul" might have disappeared from contemporary university education. While teaching a class in political philosophy, I spoke one day of the soul. A graduate student (taking his first political philosophy class) looked puzzled and said he did not know what that meant, and asked what "the modern word" for that would be.

One need not suggest that anything that could have been taught to the NIU shooter in a university would have cured whatever ailed him. Perhaps the most that could have conceivably been done would have been to try to encourage him to love, and be attracted to, the good and the beautiful. This attempt would at least have recognized that the struggle between attraction to the good and beautiful, and attraction to evil, brutality, horror and ugliness, is part of the struggle typical of the human soul. And that education might have mitigated the attraction to horror, brutality, and ugliness which the tattoos suggest. And if even *that* was not possible, at least the right kind of education could have taught him that it is not a matter of indifference to the rest of us that he spent time gazing into the abyss by reading certain of Nietzsche's books which are likely to intensify these ugly longings that the ancients would have called "tyrannical." An education aimed at forming a healthy soul would not make it a matter of indifference if students immersed themselves in *The Anti-Christ* or *Beyond Good and Evil*.

But then again, perhaps educated people no longer know, or agree, what a healthy soul is.[10]

MENS SANA IN CORPORE SANO

By way of reflecting on what "the idea of the American university" might entail, let me first reflect on that idea as I experienced it in a Catholic men's liberal arts college between 1959 and 1962. That is, before the revolution which I will describe.

Academically, the college required all students to have a minor in philosophy (12 hours). This meant 12 hours of textbooks teaching Thomism according to the Dominicans. The courses were pretty much required each semester: formal logic, ethics, speculative philosophy and metaphysics. This requirement had the effect of making philosophical thinking a central part of everyone's education. It facilitated and created some commonality of students' intellectual interests. It enabled us go out into the hall of our dorms and engage in a somewhat focused conversation. We had enough readings and topics in common to do that.

A foreign language was required of all students. Latin and Greek were encouraged but the concession that "modern languages" *were* foreign languages had already been won earlier in the 20th century. Thus, while classical learning was still a significant part of our collective experience, it was no longer a universal experience for all students at that college, much less for all American college students.[11] I did not understand why this mattered until much later when I learned from Tocqueville that in Greek and Latin writers,

> Nothing is written hurriedly or casually, but is always intended for connoisseurs and is always seeking an ideal beauty. No other literature puts in bolder relief just those qualities democratic writers tend to lack, and therefore no other literature is better to be studied at such times. This study is the best antidote against the inherent defects of the times, whereas the good qualities natural to the age will blossom untended. . . they have special merits well calculated to counterbalance our peculiar defects. They provide a prop just where we are most likely to fail.[12]

Faculty defenders of the liberal education of that time still quoted the Latin aphorism *mens sana in corpore sano*—that the mind be sound in a sound body.[13] A concern for the sound mind suffused the curriculum. The Latin I studied included Cicero's books *On Friendship, On Old Age,* and *On Duties.* While we learned the language, these books exposed us to merely rational, pagan wisdom about what a good life was. This was in addition to the required religion course each semester and the required philosophy courses. The cumulative effect of these requirements was to make serious reflection on the good life central to the curriculum.

The college tried to encourage the sound body aspect *partly* by requiring all of us to do "physical education" each semester. Freshman took a two semester class. After that, we were required to participate each semester in intramural sports (touch football, softball, basketball, soccer, golf, etc.). There were specific requirements for such participation. For instance, one year I played golf in the Spring semester. That required playing 72 holes over the semester. I remember that because, going into the semester's last weekend, I had only played 36. To complete the requirement, I played 36 holes that Sunday, in pouring rain, after walking 1 1/2 miles to the golf course, up and down the not inconsiderable hills of Dubuque, and home again. It goes without saying that I did not have a car.

Fulfilling the physical education requirement after freshman year was largely a matter of honor because we were not supervised by a teacher. To fulfill the requirement, we had only to report what we had done and when.

For example, for golf we had to hand in the score cards. The honor which this approach both assumed and was meant to cultivate would, I suppose, have been understood as part of *sana mens*. *Mens* (mind) and *anima* (soul) overlapped a lot and frequently, and cultivating one meant cultivating the other.

There was also a broader attempt to form our character though living conditions. Underclassmen were required to live on campus and have "lights out" by a certain time. The time was 10:00 pm on week nights, and midnight on weekends. Getting a good night's sleep was thought to be important, so that students would be ready to learn the next day. I am struck by this now when my students commonly cannot get up to come to a 10:00 am class because of festivities the night before.

Another means of character formation was limiting the number of nights students could stay out until midnight. The number was dependent on the year of study. All students automatically got Friday night out until midnight. Freshmen got one additional "midnight." sophomores two additional, and juniors and seniors three. Students had to sign in at the dormitory's front desk where there was a night watchman who drew a line across the sign in sheet at midnight. Anyone who signed in after that would be disciplined by the Dean. The object was to encourage the self-discipline of getting in on time.

Juniors and seniors were permitted to live off campus, presumably on the assumption that they had learned the responsible use of their freedom from their parents' supervision.

One could say that the idea of *mens sana in corpore sano* partly aimed to uplift our souls. But it was mainly to set the conditions under which such an uplifting could occur in more substantive ways.

CIVILIZATIONAL MEMORY AND THE
UPWARD LIFTING OF SOULS

That more substantive purpose of pointing our souls upward was captured by the motto of the college: *Pro Deo et Patria*. *Pro Patria* was broadly understood and was encouraged in three required courses. Freshman year was a two semester class in European history. The clear goal was to help us understand "Western civilization" and the place of Christianity in giving rise to and sustaining it. The notion of *Patria* was thereby broader than the merely nationalistic one now common. This broader notion of *Patria* was at least partly an effect of the experience of sending two generations of American soldiers to salvage Europe in the 50 preceding years. The effect of this class on me at the time was a sense of America's rootedness in a civilization beyond America, i.e., that our *Patria* in the particular sense was not all our own work and had a broader civilizational context. This effect was intensified in me when, almost 50 years later, I first stood among the crosses and stars of David in the American cemetery at Normandy. It then came to me that the British and French boys buried nearby had been at Normandy because their countries had been attacked by the Germans. But not the American boys. Their country had not been attacked by the Germans. They were there to rid the world of Nazism and to save Western and Christian civilization.

This "Western" and certainly "Christian" language is not gratuitous, although it will seem unfamiliar today given the anti-Western and secular outlook which now fashions how our history is remembered in universities. For this memory, World War II was about saving "freedom." It was that, but it is a more complete, and therefore more accurate, "civilizational memory" to speak of saving Western and Christian Civilization.

Here is the evidence. First, and most visibly, American boys at Normandy, unlike at Arlington Cemetery, are buried under what then were, unremarkably and unashamedly, symbols of Christian civilization, namely, crosses and stars of David. Part of the evidence that these then symbolized our civilization is that Winston Churchill, the preeminent allied spokesman for what was at stake in that war, famously said "the Battle of France is over. I expect that the Battle of Britain is about to begin. Upon this battle depends the survival of Christian civilisation. Upon it depends our own British life, and the long continuity of our institutions and our Empire."[14] Churchill too had a notion of *Patria* as encompassing more than Great Britain in isolation from its broader civilizational context.

Additional evidence is that President Franklin Roosevelt went on national radio the morning after the Normandy invasion to announce to the American people that the invasion was under way and to ask them to join him in prayer for our troops and for victory. He spoke of the invasion as a "crusade."[15] Finally, the allied commander of the invasion forces, General Dwight D. Eisenhower, titled his memoir of the War *Crusade in Europe* (1948).[16]

It may not be entirely superfluous to include here the literal historical meaning of "crusade" according to the Oxford English Dictionary: "A military expedition undertaken by the Christians of Europe in the 11th, 12th, and 13th centuries to recover the Holy Land from the Muslims." Although the O.E.D. has subsequent more figurative and analogical meanings, it is still redolent of "the cross" in contrast to the more secular term "war." Anyone who doubts the persistence of the religious overtones can reflect on President George W. Bush's use of "crusade" to describe the war on terrorism at his September 16, 2001, press conference. Googling "George W. Bush" with "crusade" produces 6,690,000 hits. One can impartially say there was much "sensitivity," both domestically and world-wide, about his use of that word. In contrast, I have found no such sensitivity about its use by Churchill, Roosevelt, or Eisenhower.

The college's required sophomore course was American history, i.e., political history. The effect of this class was to try to get us to care about the Constitution and its development, with emphasis on the Civil War and Lincoln's presidency. The required junior class was "Catholic Socio-Economic Principles." Since America was somewhat lacking from the point of view of encyclicals like *Rerum Novarum* and *Quadragesimo Anno* and its descendants, the question of how "*Patria*" might be reformed so as to be closer to "*Deo*" was a lively topic of teaching, discussion and debate in this class.

In sum, "civilizational memory" then meant Western, Christian and American civilization.

FORMING CHARACTER, BODY AND MIND IN THE PRE-REVOLUTIONARY SECULAR STATE UNIVERSITY

When I began teaching at Northern Illinois University in 1966, some of the character-forming structure discussed above was in place there. There were rules governing student life which reflected recognizable ideas of "good behavior" which perhaps might lead to "good character." The legal rubric under which the university took seriously its character forming role was *in loco parentis.*

Most students in practice—and all freshmen and sophomores by regulation—lived on campus, which was a necessary condition for effective *in loco parentis.* The dormitories had "parietal hours."[17] Men and women lived in separate dorms, or in separate wings of the same building, and there were rules governing men being in women's dorms. An important parietal was that women had to be in their dorm rooms by midnight—a policy designed to give at least some encouragement to chastity, as well as to regular sleep time. Giving support to students developing regular habits, even regarding morally neutral matters such as sleep, was, of course, one of the traditional means of moral education of the young. Indirectly, but effectively, requiring women to be in by midnight also had a salutary effect on the male students who then tended to return to their separate dorms.

There was also a dress code for both sexes, which aimed at inculcating modesty as well as an orderly appearance. The idea might have been that one had a responsibility to present oneself in a decent and orderly manner for the sake of others. This "other-regarding" code was enforced primarily in the cafeteria food lines. The women running the line did more than check ID's to be sure you were a student and entitled to be eating there; if they thought your dress inappropriate, you didn't eat until you passed inspection.

There was a Dean of Men and Dean of Women responsible for enforcing various rules governing behavior, both academic and personal. Many of the personal behavioral rules, which were not limited to academic integrity, were likewise to encourage concern for others.

For the body, in addition to encouraging getting regular and sufficient sleep, there were 4 semesters of required Physical Education, largely intramurals. Even this had separate classes for men and women.

The character forming *in loco parentis* rules were swept away by the cultural revolution that occurred in this and most other American universities, as well as American society at large, between 1967 and 1972. Parietal hours were abolished, men could be in the women's dorms at any time, the dress code disappeared, men and women took physical education together. In general, the university's attempt to instill the idea that goodness involved self-discipline regarding pleasure seeking and orderliness in dress and sleep habits, was replaced by the idea that goodness meant opposing the Vietnam war and supporting civil rights.

NIU also then had a somewhat coherent substantive notion of what an educated person should know. As late at the 1969–70 Catalog, all students were required to take two semesters of writing and English Literature, a Math course, four semesters of Physical Education and a Speech class. There were also a certain number of hours required from among a list of classes in Sciences, Humanities, and Social Sciences. And they were required to either take a class in, or pass an examination, on the principles of the American Constitution and Declaration of Independence, and the Illinois Constitution.

By the 1974–75 Catalog, Physical Education had been done away with as the university abandoned the idea than an educated person have a *"corpore sano."* While the specific English, Math and Speech classes remained, there was a 39 percent reduction in the number of hours required in Science (from 11–12 to 7); in Humanities (from 15 to 9), and Social Science (from 9 to 6).

The principles governing these revisions in "distribution requirements" were opaque. Faculty discussed them in terms of protecting the "credit hour production" of individual departments (the basis of budgetary allocations) without reference to any ideas of what it was hoped the educational effects would be on students. The closest one could come to formulating a principle for the revisions was that individual choice, rather than any substantive idea of educational outcome, was given greater prominence than previously.[18]

The best evidence for the foregoing interpretation is the following. Until 1971–72, the Undergraduate Catalog had begun the General Education section with this quote. "A liberal education . . . is the education which gives a man a clear, conscious view of his own opinions and judgments, a truth in developing them, an eloquence in expressing them, and a force in urging them." Followed by "The General Education section of a student's undergraduate program is especially designed to contribute to liberal education as defined above by John Henry Newman."[19] That quote disappeared from the 1974–75 catalog and was replaced by the following: "The general education requirements may be met by transfer credit, course proficiency examination or advanced placement, as well as by regular credit."

The hypothesis that merely formal *choice* had replaced *substance* would explain this change. Liberal education disappeared even in name and was replaced by choice. What General Education course requirements remained said to students, in effect, two things: 1) "we want you to learn the skills of speaking, writing and calculating but we do not care about the substance of what you choose to speak, write or calculate" and 2) "learn a little of this and a little of that" but less than we previously wanted you to learn.

Prior to the revolution, there had been the evidence cited above for my state university's curricular commitment to cultivating what were recognizably liberally educated human beings, that is, of forming their thought, their speech, their principles, their judgment, and their instincts. In a word, forming their *souls*, especially about what it meant for educated people to live well, and more especially about how we should live well *together*. This kind of education implied therefore that human beings had souls, that these souls could be at least partly cultivated by education, and that questions such as "what is a healthy human soul" and "what kind of family, society, and political community best fosters them," were meaningful, important, and could be answered in better, as distinguished from worse, ways. And finally that the study of these things was central to any "higher" form of education.

After the revolution, that is by the 1974–75 catalog, that evidence virtually disappeared. In retrospect, it seems that disappearance, and the corresponding disappearance of the character forming rules and requirements for student living, looks like evidence that the faculty and administration no longer agreed about what it meant to be educated.

UPWARD MOBILITY IN THE
POST-REVOLUTIONARY UNIVERSITY

Public universities had always had an important "upward mobility" motivation which was in some tension with the character forming, civilizational memory instilling, soul uplifting purposes of being "educated." The public university's job, when I entered it in 1966, was to take students who came for economic reasons and shove an education in front of them in hopes of lifting their sights a bit. When the latter disappeared during and after the late 1960s, what remained of "the idea of the American university" was upward mobility.

Specifically, the post-revolutionary curriculum no longer commonly required European or even American history; classical languages all but disappeared and certainly no longer made a decisive impact on the collective university culture; Deo and Patria as organizing commitments similarly vanished as secularism consolidated its hold and attachment to country was displaced by various internationalisms. The curriculum, like the new conditions of student life, came to be governed by individual choice mitigated by an institutional interest in assuring that all Departments got a share of the credit hours. The resulting "idea of the American university" could be fairly characterized by a culinary metaphor: "a cafeteria." Students increasingly came to college simply to pursue the democratic regime inspired idea of getting ahead, to get a better job than their fathers had, to move from the working class to the middle class, or from middle to upper class. The old idea that "education" should form ones character, teach students to "look up" to models of healthy souls derived from the wisest thinkers of our civilization, did not have much interest for students satisfied (as Tocqueville thought typical of democracies) that the good life consisted in material abundance. What interested them was knowledge, or at least certification, that could be sold in the marketplace. The remnant of the old learning, which came to be called "general education," was a set of requirements, so unintelligible to them that they were merely to be "gotten out of the way" so one could get onto ones major.

While the faculty and institutions were abandoning the pre-revolutionary idea of a university, they were simultaneously re-fashioning universities according to their self-interest. One example has to do with money. Historically, one did not become a university faculty member for the purpose of earning much money. On the contrary, such a life in any university required an element of economic self-sacrifice, most emphatically in religious universities.[20] One chose this life for the non-economic rewards of being able, as a way of life, to pursue the study of what one loved and to share that love with the next generation. It was a vocation. And one was grateful if one found at least some students willing and eager to receive the bread which one cast, trustingly and hopefully, upon the waters.[21] But salaries began to rise dramatically in the 1960s and thereafter. Among other things, this bought into universities, especially public universities, people oriented to their "career" rather than to their vocation. Faculty became upwardly mobile too. Instead of a long term commitment to their institution, they increasingly became committed to their "profession"; and "profession" did not mean teaching but visibility in their chosen field of research and publishing outside their university. Such visibility enabled them to aspire to move to a more prestigious university with corresponding economic and status rewards. "National reputation" became a norm governing institutional promotion and tenure.

AN APPARENT DIGRESSION ON HOW HEALTHY THE PRE-REVOLUTIONARY UNIVERSITY ACTUALLY WAS

Lest I give the impression that the revolution upended an altogether healthy idea of the American university, let me modify that by recounting a speech which profoundly influenced me as a college Freshman. It was written by Adolf A. Berle, Jr.[22] Berle had been one of FDR's leading "brain trusters" and had already had a distinguished career. At the time of this speech he was Professor of Law at Columbia University.[23] Rereading the speech now is instructive about the pre-revolutionary ideas which Berle thought had come to dominate the American university. He says "the first and deepest issue" of the 1960s is that

> universities and American intellectuals have, I am clear, been running away from the greatest and most constant of all human issues. This is, quite simply, whether life has an enduring significance, or whether it is an anarchy of chance, meaning nothing. Properly, this should have been the concern of the Departments of Philosophy in our universities. Yet so far as I recall, the last great study of eternal values in the United States was published by Hugo Muensterberg of Harvard—who died in 1916. Nor have historians and social scientists filled the gap, though some of them have tackled fragments of it. England's Toynbee has had the courage to make the attempt to make a philosophy of history, whether one agrees with it or not. Sociologists describe–and commonly let it go at that. Economists set out the result of human wants. None of these have dealt with the primary question of values.[24]

Berle is emphatic that American society and universities are in a "moral crisis" with which they refuse to come to grips. The moral crisis involves "foreign affairs," the "world economic system," American "self-indulgence," the need for a "far higher degree of personal conscientiousness" and "intense personal responsibility . . . in every expression of life." The specific evils he mentions are "payola" or private bribery and the extent to which that may have corrupted "mass communication" and "advertising media"; the connection between "cheating in school, misreporting on income tax returns and corruption in commercial and public life"; and "commercially 'planned' or 'designed' obsolescence." The cumulative impact of these "evils," as he pointedly calls them, is to call into question "where have parents, teachers, professors, schools, and colleges been all this time"? Or "where were the men trained who accepted this perversion of values"?[25]

He draws the conclusion that "bluntly, universities everywhere ought to concern themselves with a moral order. In academic lingo this is called a value system." He explicates what that should look like and concludes, "I hold it the task of the universities, guardians of our intellectual dynamo, to give definition, form and intellectual leadership in developing the new social concepts and the new measures we obviously need."[26]

Two of my professors, Father Robert Ferring, a political scientist, and Father Francis Friedl, a psychologist, heard this speech. They found it so exciting that they gathered together a group of students to discuss it in a formal and structured way. We met regularly from March 15 until the end of the Spring semester 1960.

If Berle is right, then my previous description of the idea of the pre-revolutionary American university as committed to character formation and uplifting souls would have to be qualified. Evidently, my recollections of my experiences are not quite as clear as they might be. A possible explanation is that, perhaps between 1959 and 1962, I experienced one of the remaining redoubts of the less-corrupted, pre-revolutionary university. This would make sense if the generality of American universities were, as Berle describes them, further advanced in the practice of avoiding teaching students "a moral order" and a sound "hierarchy of values." Perhaps my college's "idea" remained protected longer because of its religious commitments.

But protected from what? Let me propose an answer. Berle's argument is that American universities were failing to recognize the "moral crisis" of the 1960s and to confront the question of the right or best "standard of values" and "value system" for their students and for American society. He does not attempt to explain this failure, only to record and denounce it.

A few years later, I think I learned the idea which largely accounts for this failure of American universities from reading Leo Strauss' *Natural Right and History* (1953). Strauss argued that "Western thought in general" had, over the course of the 27 years preceding *Natural Right and History*[27] been taken over by "unqualified relativism" stemming from "the historical sense" created by German thought. I take it he means Nietzsche via the Heidegger spawned existentialism and Weber's fact/*value* distinction. If "values" are nothing but "will to power," rather than knowledge of that which is good, true, and just everywhere and always, then the only "standard of values" is the will of the stronger. So there is no "value system" or "hierarchy of values" to teach. The strong will take what they wish and the weak will yield what they must. So there is nothing for education to do to resist that.[28]

In this same paragraph, Strauss acknowledges that one kind of "Western thought" has remained exempt from "unqualified relativism" namely "Roman Catholic social science." This would seem to support the speculation above that the Catholic college I attended may have been "one of the remaining redoubts of the uncorrupted, pre-revolutionary university."

In another place Strauss explains the effect triumphant relativism must have on its opponents. Relativism seems to exalt individual choice and hence tolerance of all choices. However, "absolute tolerance is altogether impossible; the allegedly absolute tolerance turns into ferocious hatred of those who have stated clearly and most forcefully that there are unchangeable standards founded in the nature of man and the nature of things."[29]

This "dogmatism based on relativism" is still dogmatism because it is based on will to power rather than on a hierarchy of values informed by these unchangeable standards. So it is less liberal education than indoctrination or bullying.

It seems to me that the triumph of relativism adequately explains the failed "idea of the American university" Berle articulates. As relativism came in the 1940s, 50s, and 60s to supplant older ideas of individual responsibility, conscientiousness, and concern for the common good, in both Western thought and in American universities, it undermined those older ideas. This adequately explains these universities' failure to perform the character forming purpose Berle pleads for.

This phenomenon of which Berle complains, as well as its cause, had been described by C. S. Lewis a generation before his 1960 speech: "You can hardly open a periodical without coming across the statement that what our civilization needs is more 'drive,' or 'dynamism,' or 'self-sacrifice,' or 'creativity.' We remove the organ and demand the function. We make men without chests and expect of them virtue and enterprise. We laugh at honour and are shocked to find traitors in our midst. We castrate and bid the geldings be fruitful."[30]

In this metaphor, the "organ" is the chest, the seat of spiritedness according to the Platonic structure of the soul. The chest (the seat of spiritedness) mediates between the head (the place of reason) and the belly (the place of the desires). The desires care only about getting pleasure and avoiding pain. In this they are short sighted because reason's foresight knows that some pleasures harm us and some pain is good for us. But reason is incapable of persuading the passions of that. However, it can persuade and hence moderate spiritedness, i.e. boldness, daring, courage, endurance of suffering and anger, the characteristic ways spiritedness manifests itself. And, in alliance with spiritedness, reason can rule the desires. But reason's capacity to guide spiritedness is undermined by "removing the organ" (the chest) which one does by teaching reason that the good, the true and the beautiful are relative, i.e. subjective opinion not knowledge.

Since Berle was no relativist, he could reasonably criticize universities for doing nothing to educate individual Americans, especially powerful ones, and most especially the economically powerful, about the "moral crisis" caused by their aggrandizing themselves at the expense of the common good.

But if relativism had, during the previous two generations, already undermined educated people's confidence that they have knowledge of what the common good is, and that they knew how to educate students to love the good and the beautiful so as to lead them to a sound "hierarchy of values," then the universities of 1960 lacked the ability to teach students what educated people no longer knew.

I cannot show that the remaking of the idea of the American university in light of individual choice in life-style and course work, upward mobility, and relativism, are all connected. I can only say that, as someone who lived through it, these ideas coincided in the revolution. Whether there is any inner connection in virtue of which they had to go together, is beyond what I know.

REMEMBRANCE OF THINGS PAST

In my 50 years in universities, the idea of the American university became much more like what Tocqueville described all democratic education as being. This would seem to mean that the non- or anti-democratic elements which I had experienced have substantially disappeared. I hope the stories from my own experience have illustrated concretely some major steps in the "going down" of the idea of a higher education of the mind, soul and body. Finally, I hope I have identified some of the causes and circumstances which brought American universities into closer congruence with democratic society as Tocqueville understood it. If so then the relativism which became ascendant in the 1940s–1960s and the cultural revolution of 1968–1974 were not *accidental* causes of the "going down" of higher education. They were essentially an outgrowth of the American democratic regime.

When I began making notes for this chapter, I wrote that I should try to find something hopeful since it is not good for ones' soul to focus too much on what has been corrupted, destroyed or lost. It is necessary to remember these things but neither necessary nor good to remember only them. While I did not dream of proposing systemic solutions, I hoped at least to remember, for myself and my readers, something like the hope reflected in the poetry of Canadian Colonel John McCrae, writing about the aftermath of the battles of Flanders. Col. McCrae looked out on the desolation in the wake of the second battle of Ypres, which was so great that all trees and almost all vegetation had been destroyed, even the grass. And yet he could just see lovely red flowers emerging "between the crosses row on row" where many of his comrades lay buried. The poppies gave hope that life could emerge even within such devastation.[31]

The devastation of what was, within my lifetime, the opportunity for a liberal education of the body and the soul in the love of intelligible ideas of the good and the beautiful, survives here and there in American universities; usually in what are today called Great Books programs or, less commonly, University Honors programs. And there are still a very few serious Great Books colleges, and some serious religious colleges where it can happen. But for large swaths of what are called universities and colleges today, the opportunity is gone, at least as far as the institutions are concerned. Let me cite two pieces of evidence. As John A. Flower, former President of Cleveland State University, has remarked

The millions of first-generation undergraduates now in mass-market institutions, like regional state universities and community colleges, have had little to no exposure to the power of thought within the liberal arts. They have no great interest in the life of the mind. The lack of experience on the part of these students in how to handle ideas—as contrasted to the immediate, hedonistic response of their senses—is both a national disgrace and a disaster. The inherent contradictions are highlighted by the billions of dollars spent on their "education'" in the public schools. These students desperately need the influence of the proven great thinkers of the past. They are not getting it.[32]

Obviously, no education in ideas means no liberal education aimed at remembering a moral order and at producing in students a thoughtful hierarchy of values.

In 2003, I was one of two outside evaluators asked to review the political science program at a large Midwestern public university. This university's website understandably cites the descriptor "Public Ivy" given to it by others.[33] So it would not seem likely to fit Flower's description of a "mass market institution." Yet, in the course of talking with a group of undergraduate majors, we found a surprisingly broad agreement about the lack of serious study of ideas in the curriculum. One student said that political science here is "pragmatic and doesn't deal with ideas." So she said she had taken a second major in women's studies because "at least they take ideas seriously." Several others commented to the effect that "at no point has there been any study of ideas that have shaped the country, of the differences between liberalism and conservatism, or the thought of the Founders, Jefferson, Lincoln or contemporary political leaders." Another student commented that "this university needs deep learning rather than superficial learning and that is what we miss from the absence of ideas in most of our political science classes." Several specifically mentioned by name the lack of "political philosophy."

When we asked these students what had made them aware of this lack, one impressive young woman stated that she had had an internship in Washington the previous Summer where she met students from Ivy league and other "good schools," and she felt "inferior" because they were conversant in these matters, and she was not. Other students reported that friends of theirs attended colleges where political ideas *were* taught and that they could only listen to their conversations since they had little to contribute from what they had been taught at their public university.[34]

Given these findings, one may reasonably wonder where one might find grounds for the hope I began by reminding myself to look for. Let me try this. If "the idea of the American university" no longer can have an agreed upon focus and structure because, relativism having done its work, educated people no longer agree about what it means to be educated, then the institutional problem is unsolvable. But at the sub-institutional level individual teachers, here and there, can keep alive what the tradition of liberal learning once understood education to be. They can do that by writing papers like the present one and sharing them with others. They can seek out individual students they encounter—the ones who love to think—and show them what liberal learning can be and how it either fulfills the individual and social need for, or at least makes possible, a well thought out hierarchy of values. And they can be open to students who come to their office or classes dissatisfied with what they are being taught and seeking something "more." They can promote the serious study of serious ideas about how we should live.

There is no *system* in this and for those who hope for systemic solutions, it is not much. For the rest of us, it is the hope engendered by our own experience of the serious study of ideas occasionally stubbornly peeking, poppy-like, through the surrounding devastation. But is this not better than acquiescing in gazing into the abyss?

This hope depends on there being teachers in universities like Colonel McCrae who are capable of noticing that the devastation is not quite complete. They will need to have something of a missionary mentality, partly because they will be mostly alone and partly because they will live in the kind of places to which civilized countries used to send missionaries. *Primis Tenebris Erunt Custodes Luminis.* The hope also depends on there being students aware of the curricular and moral devastation surrounding them and being drawn to the light which such teachers struggle to keep from flickering out altogether. And finally it depends on such teachers and students finding each other, more or less—but not entirely, as we believe—by chance.

NOTES

1. Alexis de Tocqueville, *Democracy in America,* ed. J. P. Mayer (New York: Harper and Row, 1969), 55.
2. de Tocqueville, *Democracy in America,* 476–77.
3. de Tocqueville, *Democracy in America,* 456.
4. de Tocqueville, *Democracy in America,* 465. Consider this observation about love of beauty where that comes up again below in part I.
5. de Tocqueville, *Democracy in America,* chapter 10, "Why the Americans are more concerned with the applications than with the theory of science," 462.
6. de Tocqueville, *Democracy in America,* 459–65.
7. de Tocqueville, *Democracy in America,* 460–61.
8. *Chicago Sun-Times,* February 20, 2008, by Dave McKinney, Annie Sweeney, and Natasha Korecki, www.highbeam.com/doc/1N1-11EF1F93D851FB90.html. The original source is Friedrich Nietzsche, *Beyond Good and Evil,* chapter IV, Apophtegms [sic] and Interludes #146. Helen Zimmern trans., Project Guttenberg Etext (2003), available at www.gutenberg.org/dirs/etext03/bygdv10.txt.
9. By Lindsey Tanner and Caryn Rousseau, *The Associated Press,* Posted February 18, 2008, www.rrstar.com/archive/x1907839958
10. See the conclusion—Remembrance of Things Past—below.
11. As a student of Latin, I remember the following put-down from that time: "Question, What is a Latinist? Answer, Someone not smart enough to do Greek." This was probably not spread by Latin students.
12. de Tocqueville, *Democracy in America,* 476–77.
13. From Juvenal, *Satire X.* Line 356 of this 366 line prayer in the form of a poem, says "orandum est ut sit mens sana in corpore sano." "It is to be prayed that the mind be sound in a sound body." The broad theme of this poem/prayer is that we humans do not know whether the things we commonly regard as good, (health, wealth, beauty, etc) will really be good for us. Therefore ask the gods. Hence, the subjunctive "is to be prayed." N. Rudd, E. C. Courtney, eds., *Juvenal: Satires I, III, X* (Latin Edition), 34. The idea that the *goal* of education should be "mens sana in corpore sano," meaning that a healthy body is necessary to a healthy mind, is a claim to know more than Juvenal claims to know. Juvenal limits himself to advising that "it is to be prayed

for" that one have both and that both will be a blessing to one. (www.amazon.com/gp/reader/0906515033/ref=sib_dp_pt#reader-link). Juvenal here follows Xenophon's Socrates who "when he prayed he asked simply for good gifts," without specifying them, because "the gods know best what things are good." *Memorabilia*, Bk. 1, Ch. iii, sec. 2. He also so counseled "many of his companions"; for "the deepest secrets" concerning the consequences of many (not all) important human actions "the gods reserved to themselves." I..i.3-9. E. C. Marchant, trans., Xenophon *Memorabilia and Oeconomicus* (Cambridge, MA: Harvard U.P. Loeb Classical Library, 1959). In particular, when Xenophon himself asked Socrates for advice about whether he should accept an invitation to join the younger Cyrus in an expedition into Persia to try to take the throne from Cyrus' brother, Socrates "advised Xenophon to go to Delphi and there to consult the god as to the desirability of such a journey." Xenophon *Anabasis*, Book III, I., 6–7.

14. "Their Finest Hour," June 18, 1940, in the House of Commons available at the Churchill Centre website 9www.winstonchurchill.org/i4a/pages/index .cfm?pageid=418).

15. Available at the website of the Franklin Delano Roosevelt Presidential Library and Museum (www.fdrlibrary.marist.edu/odddayp.html).

16. I have not found "crusade" used to describe the war against Japan. One might speculate that the explanation might be that the war against Japan was merely traditional power politics to prevent being ruled by another country; whereas Naziism meant to replace Christian civilization with a way of life which transvalued Christianity in a thoroughgoing manner.

17. I am given to believe "parietal" may no longer be familiar language to younger readers. The O.E.D. defines it as "Relating to or designating the regulations governing residence of students within a college, *esp.* those which restrict or prohibit visits from members of the opposite sex."

18. The required instruction in government and the Constitution was kept because of a statutory mandate. However, in 1987 the University abandoned the requirement, following the lead of the University of Illinois. The statute remains in place but unenforced. Thus disappeared the last substantive (i.e. not merely formal) idea in the curriculum about what an educated person should know.

19. p. 21.

20. A wealthy businessman relative of mine said to me, during this time, "Gary, I do not understand why someone with your brains and your education is willing to work for peanuts." This man was kindly disposed to me, actively cared about me and had been generous in helping me secure a Ph.D. He was not being nasty but only expressing a perplexity understandable from someone for whom "life is a game and money is how you keep score." His formulation.

21. Now that so few in universities recognize Biblical passages, one can even use this language expressing faith and trust from Ecclesiastes 11 without being suspected of smuggling religious ideas into the university.

22. The title is "The Irrepressible Issues of the 60's" and was given to the "Opening General Session of the Fifteenth National Conference on Higher Education," March 9,

1960. I do not know if it was ever published. I have it in the typed form which presumably Berle provided the conference. It is a mere 5 1/2 single spaced pages long.

23. A competent biography is Jordan Schwarz, *Liberal: Adolf A. Berle and the Vision of an American Era* (Free Press, 1987). Schwarz summarizes Berle's contribution to New Deal thought thusly: "Big corporations should be regulated by a supreme national power in Washington that liberated Americans from economic oligarchy and broadened wealth without altering the essentials of American individualism. Berle was an effective advocate of 'collectivist' capitalist planning and one of the most heralded radicals of the depression decade."

24. Berle, 3.

25. Compare Berle's assumption that "teachers, professors, schools and colleges" would be questioned as to why they did not at least attempt to produce students who had good character, with the absence of this question regarding the NIU shooter (see above section 1). That Berle's question is no longer being asked suggests that the now 4th generation of relativism influenced higher education has led to the questions' disappearance.

26. Berle, 4, 5.

27. The lectures which became *Natural Right and History* were delivered in 1951. So "27 years" explicitly refers to the 1934 publication date of "Ernst Troeltsch on Natural law and Humanity" in Otto Gierke, *Natural Law and the Theory of Society*. Strauss says Troeltsch's description of German thought as "unqualified relativism" has come, in the intervening [27] years, to apply to "Western thought in general." See *Natural Right and History* (1953), 1–2.

28. Strauss says the 27 years in which German relativism triumphed in the West includes the years when Germany was militarily defeated and even "annihilated as a political being." Strauss notes that this "would not be the first time that a nation" so defeated, "has deprived its conquerors of the most sublime fruit of victory by imposing on them the yoke of its own thought." See *Natural Right and History*, 2.

29. "The Liberalism of Classical Political Philosophy" in *Liberalism: Ancient and Modern* (New York: Basic Books, 1968) p. 63. Originally published in *Review of Metaphysics*, XII, No. 3 (March 1959), 390–439.

30. C. S. Lewis, *The Abolition of Man* (1943), the last paragraph of chapter 1, "Men Without Chests."

31. "In Flanders Fields" (1915). McCrae was a Canadian doctor who tended the wounded on the Western Front in The Great War.

32. *The Chronicle of Higher Education*, November 21, 2003, chronicle.com/weekly/v50/i13/13b01301.htm. This article is excerpted from Flower's book *Downstairs, Upstairs: The Changed Spirit and Face of College Life in America*, published by University of Akron Press (2003). I do not know if Pres. Flower is especially enamored of poppies.

33. "The 2007 edition of *The Insider's Guide to the Colleges* describes Miami as a Public Ivy that 'takes education seriously.'" "Miami was named one of 30 schools in the United States that offers 'an education comparable to that at Ivy League universities at a fraction of the price' in the book *The Public Ivies: America's Flagship*

Universities." From the school's website: www.miami.muohio.edu/about_miami/ recognition/

34. The preceding two paragraphs, including the quotes, are from my post-visit report written in December 2003.

35. With apologies to William Bennett, "Does Honor Have a Future"? *Imprimis*, December 1998, www.hillsdale.edu/news/imprimis/archive/issue.asp?year=1998& month=12.

4

Roller of Big Cigars

The American University as Cheerful Mortician

Peter Wood

"Roller of Big Cigars" comes from the opening line of a poem by Wallace Stevens. The poem is not about higher education or the university, and thus I assume the duty of showing that it has some appositeness to the topic at hand.

The roller of big cigars is a small town mortician, and he has been called in to a house to prepare the corpse of an unlovely woman, a seamstress perhaps, who died at home in the midst of busyness. The circumstances might sound unpromising, even shabby, but Stevens dresses them grandiloquently, and in the imperative:

The Emperor of Ice-Cream

Call the roller of big cigars,
The muscular one, and bid him whip
In kitchen cups concupiscent curds.
Let the wenches dawdle in such dress
As they are used to wear, and let the boys
Bring flowers in last month's newspapers.
Let be be finale of seem.
The only emperor is the emperor of ice-cream.
Take from the dresser of deal.
Lacking the three glass knobs, that sheet
On which she embroidered fantails once
And spread it so as to cover her face.
If her horny feet protrude, they come
To show how cold she is, and dumb.
Let the lamp affix its beam.
The only emperor is the emperor of ice-cream.[1]

55

Fortunately it is not my task to explicate this poem, but only to pillage it. The roller of big cigars, the muscular one, isn't a fellow of grace and refinement. He is just the guy who can get the job done, and he goes about his work with an undimmed lust for life, and perhaps just plain lust for the dawdling wenches. Why else are the curds in his morticians' make-up kit concupiscent? In any case, he is a realist about the situation. The lady is cold and dumb.

The roller of big cigars dates back to an earlier time in American life when morticians made house calls, but he also represents an attitude and personality that is still with us and still recognizably American. He may lack finesse; he may be a bit vulgar; but he is reliable and up to the task. I nominate him as the presiding spirit of the contemporary American university, of the institution as a whole.

That is to say, I don't think we have an *idea* of the American university, but we have in its stead a sensibility. That it is a coarse and crude sensibility might be unfortunate, but it is also a muscular one and plenty able to get the job done. At least as long as we are willing to define the job of higher education as applying morticians' make-up to the corpse of Western civilization and otherwise making the old bird presentable for a family viewing.

I don't intend to blame this situation on any one party. The roller of big cigars in my metaphor is not university administrators, Leftist faculties, or careerist students. The roller of big cigars is the university itself.

The American university has become too big, too administrative, too diffuse, too fractured, too pluralistic, too unaccountable, too corrupted, too legalistic, and withal too expensive to have a genuine idea of itself. It has instead a marketing plan. The elevation of mind and the formation of character aren't part of that plan; and neither are the civic virtues that sustain a free society. Innovation and discovery, however, still have a place at least as part of well-run grants, contracts, and intellectual property programs.

There are no doubt particular colleges that run against the temper of the times and still seek to develop mind and character, civic virtue, self-discipline, civilized humanity, knowledge, innovation, and a meaningful path for the future that steers clear of the wild enthusiasms of the moment. But these hold-outs from the Best Buy/Walmart model of higher ed are by no stretch the idea of the American university. They are just speed bumps in the parking lot.

The roller of big cigars is not to be despised for who he is or what he does. He's just doing his honest work with a cheerful attitude, not unlike the gravedigger in *Hamlet*. But speaking of *Hamlet*, you have heard a ghost of him sneaking across the stage in one line: "Let be be finale of seem," commands Stevens rather cryptically. The line echoes a bit of Hamlet's "to be or not to be" soliloquy and also that moment when Hamlet tells his mother his grief is real, "Seems, Madam! Nay it is; I know not 'seems.'" But this is small town America, not Elsinore in gloomy old Denmark, and the tone is robustly positive, not existentially whiny. Stevens is the American poet whose poems often compound plain and extravagant language, and imbue ordinary scenes with yearning for the sublime. "Let be be finale of seem," has a grand and rousing sound to it, but it occurs smack in the middle of a short poem about an ordinary death. Roughly it summons us to accept things as they are. Accept reality for what it is, despite the disappointments.

But it's not a fatalistic, "Let it be." "Let be be finale of seem" is exuberant. It is a finale with a flourish. The next line of the poem continues the exuberant tone with a defiantly death-be-not-proud conceit:

Let be be finale of seem
The only emperor is the emperor of ice-cream.

If that seems rather sacrilegious, remember we've invited the roller of big cigars, not the Catholic priest or the Methodist minister to attend to this work. And it may well be that the wenches in their everyday clothes and the boys with the flowers in last month's newspapers are more interested in today's ice cream than yesterday's old biddy.

The American university, having long since shaken off any serious interest in the otherworldly, in God, in metaphysics, and in theology, gets on with its practical tasks and its plain enjoyment of life. It isn't necessarily opposed to people dabbling in higher sorts of things. It even has chaplains on campus and its own chapel, as well as courses in comparative religion. But concupiscence is, all told, a lot more interesting. That's why we have mandatory safe-sex training in freshman orientation, a full suite of gender studies and gay studies courses in the curriculum, a sex column in the student newspaper, *and* sexual harassment training for the faculty. We're thinking a lot about "the body" these days. No, not that toe-tagged corpse of Western civ, the other body, the warm one that is receptive to all the *qualia* of this wonderful universe.

And we don't want to intellectualize this experience too much. In fact, if we seek to understand the university in America as it is right now, we need to observe how much the roller of big cigars, the muscular one, has swapped out intellectual inquiry and swapped in social activities, emotional adjustment, and commitment to community. On most campuses, the office of student life has more than doubled in size and is claiming a bigger share of time, resources, and importance. Faculty members, it is said, just teach a tiny fraction of the student and concentrate on mere cognition. Student life, by contrast, reaches out to the whole person. And whole persons are in need of emotional sustenance and therapy, as well as an understanding that their wholeness cannot be realized outside of a commitment to social justice.

Relatively few faculty members object to this sort of thing, and the result is that college is often an odd mixture of supposed job training, or at least job credentialing, supposedly therapeutic immersion in identity groups, urging students to get politically active, and, of course, a lot of partying. Does this accomplish much?

Well, says the roller of big cigars, *it gets the job done. Look at our alumni. They're doing pretty well. And plenty more students are eager to come. You can't argue with success.*

But that's not really true. You *can* argue with success if you have a mind to. You could, for example, say that the migration of the "whole person" to programs run by student life does indeed testify to the shallowness of the curriculum. If students are reading worthy books taught in a worthy way in their academic courses, their classes are by no means arid exercises in "mere cognition." I'm not sure how one could read Homer, Augustine, Dante, or Shakespeare without emotional and moral engagement, though no doubt some professors try. Why would we want to impose a division of labor where the professoriate radically depersonalizes the curriculum and another bunch of counselors step in to offer a more feelings-based sense of community? Shouldn't the community arise from the shared project of seeking an education together?

Good luck with that says the roller of big cigars. He is thinking something like this: The American university, by many yardsticks, is flourishing as never before. It has more students—some 18 million; a higher percentage of young people enrolled—some 70 percent of recent high school graduates;[2] more faculty members—over 675,000 full time and nearly as many part-time;[3] more income from tuition; more federal and state support; more research grants; more scholarly publications; and more students from abroad than at any previous time in American history. The American university also enjoys an extraordinary cultural and social position. Large numbers of Americans believe that a college degree is a prerequisite to material success. Politicians of both parties elbow each other out of the way to bestow ever-increasing public largess on universities. In the midst of our nation's economic calamity, higher education has been the recipient of about $20 billion in so-called stimulus funds, and many more billions are promised.

Of course, even a successful institution has its critics. Some on the Left complain that the university has become too corporate and too concerned with its own financial interests, and that a larger public good is scanted. Some complain that the full-time faculty, who mostly enjoy the advantages of academic freedom, are fairly quickly being replaced by legions of adjunct professors who are, on the whole, poorly paid, vulnerable to dismissal, and unable to sustain the central position of the faculty in shaping the curriculum and ethos of the university.

Another line of criticism focuses on the very high and still rising tuition and expenses of American higher education. And though private colleges and universities typically charge more than public institutions, the complaints about exorbitant tuition apply to both. Criticisms of the university's financial arrangements don't stop with tuition. Scandals involving the self-dealing of financial aid administrators, the misdoings of banks and other lenders involved in student aid, and corruption in the Department of Education have deepened the sense that higher education has acquired some of the rapacious aspects of big business.

Still another group of critics focus on the politicization of higher education and complain that American colleges and universities now generally operate with an entrenched bias against academic traditionalists and political and cultural conservatives. These critics inveigh against racial preferences in admissions; against academic appointment procedures that are biased against conservatives; against the marginalization of Western civilization in the curriculum; against the creation of new academic programs that are rooted in doctrines that reject open-minded inquiry; and against faculty members who use their classrooms with impunity to engage in partisan advocacy.

But the roller of big cigars generally shrugs off all of these criticisms. The critics go mostly unanswered, or are dismissed with gestural replies. The roller of big cigars knows his position is secure.

If the picture I am offering of the American university as self-satisfied, pragmatic, sensual, and bored with the higher things rings true, we shouldn't forget that the roller of big cigars is an artist too. He paints in the medium that Hamlet referred to when he instructed Yorick's skull, "Get you to my lady's chamber, and tell her, let her paint an inch thick." The American university does precisely this kind of painting when it presents to parents and prospective students programs of studies full of courses that sound like the liberal arts but that are actually taught as exercises in debunking great works. These courses are painted skulls, tricked out to look something like the living thing but devoid of life, light, and soul.

In conjuring the roller of big cigars, I have evaded the harder task of saying just how the cheerful mortician happened to be put in charge of one of our pivotal institutions. Did the old lady just happen to die and the roller of big cigars got called in?

I have two answers, one that draws on my work as a would-be reformer of the university, the other on my perspective as an anthropologist who studies America.

Some years ago when I was working on my book, *Diversity: The Invention of a Concept*, I found a sharp discontinuity in way the word "diversity" was used in higher education. After the 1978 U.S. Supreme Court decision in *Bakke v. The Regents of the University of California*, "diversity" was used almost exclusively to speak to the racial composition of college enrollments. Before 1978, however, when academics wrote or spoke of "diversity" in higher education, they invariably meant the variety of colleges and universities: large and small, public and private, single-sex and co-ed, research-oriented or liberal arts, secular or sectarian, selective or generally open, and so on. The idea then current was that this variety was itself the distinctive "American" characteristic of American higher education. Universities in various European nations are—or *were*, depending on how far the Bologna Process goes—allied to their national identities. American higher education was allied to American pluralism.

In the decades since, that variety has attenuated and with it the valorization of such variety is seldom pursued. There are, for example, only two single-sex male colleges left in the U.S., and a small fraction of the single-sex female colleges there were forty years ago. Variety has also attenuated as hundreds of small, formerly independent colleges were folded into state university systems. Numerous small sectarian colleges likewise closed their doors. Between 1967 and 1990, at least 167 private four-year colleges either closed or were absorbed by other institutions.[4] Besides the disappearance or reduction of certain kinds of colleges, variety was attenuated in other ways too. The Higher Education Act of 1965 created some powerful incentives for colleges to move toward some common approaches. Title IV of the Act set up a system of federally-guaranteed loans to students, requiring that students could spend the funds only at accredited colleges and universities. Very quickly accreditation went from being a relatively inconsequential exercise to an institutional prerequisite, and another force for homogenization. Similarly Title IX, barring discrimination on the basis of sex to institutions receiving Federal financial assistance, was passed in the Education Amendments of 1972, and it too became a force for homogenization.

Numerous other legislative acts, executive regulations, and judicial rulings affecting higher education have entered the picture in the years since, and no matter their intent, they have without exception favored standardization over the robust variety that once characterized the American system. The most recent attempt came from Secretary of Education Margaret Spellings who appointed a Commission on the Future of Higher Education in 2005, and proceeded to implement as much as she could of its rather robotic agenda, which aimed at establishing a federally-enforced quality-control system for higher education.

Such bureaucratic standardization, however, is not all externally imposed. Some of it comes from higher education's own herding impulse. University offices of general counsel, for example, often advise their clients that there is relative safety from lawsuits in doing things the way everyone else does. Sexual harassment training, for example, appears to have little or no effect on actual instances of sexual harassment on campus, but a college might well be in a worse position in defending itself in court against charges that it was negligent if it failed to institute such training.

The government's incentives for standardization and disincentives for independent approaches were augmented by still another development: the rapid politicization of the university starting in the 1970s and continuing to the present. Actually, if we were to pick a date at which this change commenced, perhaps the best would be the capitulation on December 8, 1964 of the University of California Berkeley Faculty Senate to the Free Speech Movement. The faculty voted 824 to 115 to adopt a resolution accepting the Free Speech Movement's claims on their face, to advise the University to take no disciplinary actions against those who rioted, and to permit the kind of advocacy that had clearly spilled over into disruption and intimidation. In effect, the efforts of radicalized students to enforce limitations on academic freedom in the name of "free speech" succeeded. To this day, American higher education continues to live in this Berkeley-invented mirror universe where "academic freedom" is routinely invoked to justify excluding views from campus. The result is ideological conformity—and yet another diminution of the institutional diversity on which American higher education once prided itself.

The apotheosis of that ideological conformity is, ironically, the new post-Bakke conception of "diversity," a doctrine that asserts the primacy of group identity over all other distinctions, and is used to enforce intellectual sameness. "Diversity" turns out to be a synonym for uniformity.

The loss of variety in higher education is one the reasons why the roller of big cigars has materialized in place of a university attuned to higher ideals. Bureaucracy and political advocacy together can never add up to a coherent vision of the university, but the combination lends itself well to a certain kind of academic careerist—a person not at home with books or ideas but who has a certain genius for catchphrases and is at ease with administrivia. Not that I want to conflate the hapless administrators chained to the idol of diversity with the roller of big cigars, who in this allegory is the whole spirit of American higher education.

My account of the shrinking institutional variety in American higher education goes only part of the way towards explaining why there is no idea of the American university. A deeper answer might be conjured from the ocean that both joins us to and separates us from Europe. America is a vast and various place, on the map and even more so in our imaginations. Columbus, who happened upon an island fringe of a continent he never encompassed, bequeathed a problem to European civilization. The encompassing of the New World was more than a problem of geography or of political rivalries among European powers. It was a problem of mind, intellectual order, moral conception, and even epistemology. The newness of the New World was not easily reconnoitered or comprehended by existing schemes. And centuries of conquest, colonization, and exploration never really sufficed to encompass all that newness, that wilderness, and that indeterminacy. Part of the effort to encompass it was to bring European institutions across the Atlantic. The results were mixed. European civilization arrived here in disaggregated form. Institutions that buttressed one another in England, in America were jostled apart.

And some institutions were, for a time, simply left home. One of these was the university. North America simply went without the university for the entire colonial period and late into the 19th century. We indeed had a form of higher education, devoted largely to the preparation of members of the clergy. Two colleges, Harvard founded in 1636, and William and Mary, in 1693, were the totality of this effort in the 17th century, and seven more were founded before the American Revolution.

The curricula of these colleges was substantially in the European tradition that had crystallized in the 1599 Jesuit plan for education, the *Ratio Studiorum,* and that had since spread to all the great universities. This meant that both the classics themselves and the classical tradition, along with history, philosophy, and literature stood in high standing and even those who did not attend college but who aspired to take part in the important conversations had read their Cicero.

With independence came an efflorescence of colleges. Nineteen more were founded by 1802 and by the civil war there were 250. But none of these colleges aspired to anything like the intellectual breadth of the English or European university, and Americans generally travelled to Europe if they sought more advanced learning.

Some early efforts to organize colleges met resistance from practical men. In the seventeenth century, petitioners in Virginia asked for a royal charter to found a college, partly on the grounds that it would help to save souls. The royal attorney general replied—so we are told—"Souls! Damn your souls! Raise tobacco!"[5] This is a view not entirely uncongenial to the roller of big cigars.

It took more than 200 years from that point to the realization in 1862 that tobacco farmers—along with other agriculturalists—could benefit from their own version of higher education. The passage of the Morrill Act, in the midst of the Civil War, created the framework for Land Grant colleges—colleges supported by sale of public land in each state. Land grant colleges realized the vision of Vermont Congressman—later Senator—Justin Morrill. Morrill was a prosperous merchant turned farmer who believed in scientific methods. You can visit his house in Strafford, Vermont today and see some of his ingenious agricultural improvements. It was in this spirit that he sought to establish, as he put it:

> at least one college in every State upon a sure and perpetual foundation, accessible to all, but especially to the sons of toil, where all of needful science for the practical avocations of life shall be taught, where neither the higher graces of classical studies nor that military drill our country now so greatly appreciates will be entirely ignored, and where agriculture, the foundation of all present and future prosperity, may look for troops of earnest friends, studying its familiar and recondite economies, and at last elevating it to that higher level where it may fearlessly invoke comparison with the most advanced standards of the world.[6]

Justin Morrill may be justly celebrated for a variety of reasons, but John Henry Newman he was not. Where Newman spoke of the university as an institution devoted to "the whole truth," based on the principles that "the various branches of science are intimately connected with each other," and in which "any considerable omission of knowledge" would "impair" the whole, Morrill happily and sometimes vehemently broke education into two pieces: the practical stuff that would prepare men for wholesome careers, and everything else, which included impractical classical learning. Fond of horticultural metaphors, he spoke of the need to prune, to "lop off a portion of the studies established centuries ago as the mark of European scholarship and replace the vacancy . . . by those of a less antique and more practical value."[7]

The utilitarian spirit of the Morrill Act became a major and eventually the dominant chord in American higher education. It can be heard throughout the 20th century from the industrial arts movement of the progressive era, through the GI Bill, and even in higher education's curricular revisions in the name of diversity intended to serve the practical function of getting college diplomas in the hands of students without the inconvenience of educating them first. Today the note is heard again in President Obama's call for every single American to attend college.

The common chord in all this is the idea that education is merely or mainly an instrumentality that should be adapted to the needs of the moment. If we need more soybean farmers, we will raise them up. More bankruptcy lawyers, place an order. More stem cell technicians, say aye.

Now clearly higher education can work this way, at least up to a point. And we have developed a body of theory that justifies the idea that the university is an endlessly reprogrammable machine that discerns and replicates a myriad of different kinds of excellence. One enthusiast called it—without irony—"an aristocracy of everyone."[8] Howard Gardner's famous theory of multiple intelligences is a clever prop to this seemingly democratic notion that education can indeed be for everyone.[9] Back in 1963, Clark Kerr enunciated the rise of the *multi-versity* as the omni-competent institution that he saw taking shape in the University of California.[10]

Kerr's prophecy, unfortunately, has been fulfilled. The utilitarian conception of higher education in America has continued to expand, and rival conceptions have continued to contract. By 1994, there were 647 self-designated liberal arts colleges, but only a third of them awarded as much as 40 percent of their degrees in the arts and sciences. The rest of the degrees were essentially vocational, in fields such as business and communications.[11] When Kerr was writing his treatise, about a quarter of college students majored in the humanities. The figure today is about 8 percent.[12]

The idea of the university, at least in its European instantiation, was an institution founded on the deep unity of knowledge. That idea, like so many others that crossed the Atlantic, was transformed on these shores. It became more a constellation of knowledge than a unity, and then fragmented still further into a congeries of knowledge with no claims of essential unity at all.

It is a liberating vision in some ways: it offers a dizzying freedom to pretend there is a plurality of little truths, each with its own epistemology, skipping past one another unhindered by contradiction. If there is an idea of the American university in that freedom, it is a university that is robust, even joyous, in the absence of intellectual constraint. The roller of big cigars has physical heft and buoyancy—and a touch of vulgarity— but his trade, of course, is prettifying the dead.

I have been answering the question, "Is there an idea of the American university?" And my answer may seem unbearably bleak. I can lighten it only so much as the illumination provided by a few Everstrike matches. Enough variety remains in the margins of American higher education that those few students who seek an education rooted in a generative vision of civilization and culture can still find it. But the larger task, that of restoring or creating anew a worthy *paideia*, a culturally central ideal of higher learning, is not something for our time. We can at best preserve the remnants of civilization in the hope that others will husband it and a wiser generation will one day see it flourish again. That doesn't mean we are off the hook. It means we carry the burden of Aeneas fleeing Troy.

A university without a core sense of the unity of knowledge is a university in which truth has died—which is to say, no university at all. Is the old lady under the sheet with the embroidered fantails truth, or civilization, or aspiration for the higher things? We're not sure. She was old, and in her later years all she did was shuffle around.

The roller of big cigars doesn't much care about the paradox that that biggest, most successful university in history is founded on makeshift ideas and collapsible premises. That's just how things are.

Let be be finale of seem
The only emperor is the emperor of ice-cream.

NOTES

1. Wallace Stevens, *The Collected Poems of Wallace Stevens* (New York: Knopf, 1972), 64. First published in *Harmonium*, 1923.

2. The figure was 63 percent in 1999, and 68 percent in 2004, according to the National Center for Education Statistics. Digest of Educational Statistics, 2007, nces. ed.gov/pubs2008/2008022_3a.pdf. A researcher at the Manhattan Institute calculated that in 2002 about 38 percent of graduating high school seniors were "college ready." Jay P. Greene, "Public High School Graduation and College-Readiness Rates: 1991–2002."

3. *The Chronicle of Higher Education*, Almanac Issue, 2008–09. August 29, 2008, 24–25.

4. Frank Oakley, Unpublished paper quoted by W. Robert Connor, "Deconstructing 'Narratives of Decline' about the Liberal Arts," February 10, 2004. Published by Project Kaleidoscope, *PKAL* Volume IV, *What Works, What Matters, What Lasts*, www.pkal.org/documents/DeconstructingNarrativesOfDecline.cfm.

5. Quoted in Christopher J. Lucas, *American Higher Education: A History* (New York. St. Martin's Griffin, 1994), 105. Original source is Herbert Baxter Adams, *The College of William and Mary* (Washington, D.C.: U.S. Bureau of Education, *Circular of Information*, no. 1, 1887), 11–15.

6. William Belmont Parker, *The Life and Public Services of Justin Smith Morrill* (Boston: Houghton Mifflin Company, 1924).

7. Parker, *The Life and Public Services of Justin Smith Morrill*. Quoted in Christopher J. Lucas, *American Higher Education: A History* (New York: St. Martin's Griffin, 1994), 147.

8. Benjamin R. Barber, *An Aristocracy of Everyone: The Politics of Education and the Future of America* (New York: Oxford University Press, 1992).

9. Howard Gardner, *Frames of Mind: The Theory of Multiple Intelligences* (New York: Basic Books, 1983).

10. Clark Kerr, *The Uses of the University*, 5th edition (1963; Cambridge: Harvard University Press, 2001).

11. Connor, op cit.

12. Eight percent is the calculation offered by the Humanities Resource Center Online, A Project of the American Academy of Arts and Sciences. See Part II,

Undergraduate and Graduate Education in the Humanities, Indicator 11-1, www .humanitiesindicators.org/content/hrcoIIA.aspx#topII1. Using a different formula, HRCO has another estimate that humanities degrees represent "12 percent of bachelor's degrees awarded in 2004." The figure has been essentially flat since 1987, down from about 17 to 16 percent in late 1960s. *The Chronicle of Higher Education* offers a higher estimate of 13.2 "Profile of Undergraduate Students, 2003-4," Almanac Issue, 2008–09, August 29, 2008, 17. Its figure derives from the National Postsecondary Student Aid Study.

5

Eccentric Education—
The American Way

Susan E. Hanssen

It is somewhat disconcerting to come across the 95 cent, 1965 Image Books edition of Christopher Dawson's *The Crisis of Western Education* now, almost half-a-century later. This valiant little paperback—with puffs from *Time* magazine and the *Saturday Review of Literature* on its cover, with an appendix touting the launch of various interdisciplinary Christian Culture programs (most now gone the way of all flesh[1]), and a blurb from Yale University professor and Christian missionary, Kenneth Scott Latourette, saying that here is "a penetrating and provocative analysis of the crisis in Western education by one of the most penetrating minds of our day"—is a paradoxical little relic of America circa 1960. It is disconcerting because as artifact Dawson's book proclaims one thing; as text, another. In its day this "complete and unabridged" secular American reprint of one of the flagship authors of Sheed & Ward, the great twentieth-century English Catholic publishing house, must have seemed to announce the official arrival of Catholic thought in America, just as Dawson's position as first Stillman Professor of Catholic Theological Studies at Harvard University and the election of John F. Kennedy seemed to signal that Roman Catholics had been freed from their immigrant ghetto and could now speak as natives in America.

The Second World War's "greatest generation" witnessed the peak of a Catholic presence in mainstream American higher education. Catholic universities in America were beginning to overcome their inferiority complex with regard to American intellectual and cultural life for a variety of reasons. The Irish were moving into the middle class and the GI Bill made it possible for more of them to choose a Catholic college than ever before. Catholics benefited from the development of the idea of "the English-speaking peoples" or the "guardians of The West"—certainly more capacious identities for Americans than the White Anglo-Saxon Protestant nativism of the turn-of-the-century. Catholic universities increased their intellectual prestige by inviting as visiting scholars the many converts who followed in John Henry Newman's steps in the second spring of English Catholicism. They could claim affinity with John Henry Newman's *Idea of a University*, and with Robert Hutchins and Mortimer Adler's insistence on the importance of the "Great Books" of the Western tradition, classical and Christian. Catholic proponents of a liberal arts training in philosophy and theology found allies amongst the WASP conservative dissidents of the modern research universities who were fighting the battle to preserve some remnant of the old classical liberal arts curriculum. It was the age of Fulton Sheen's popular television program, of John Courtney Murray's confident *We Hold These Truths* and William F. Buckley's glowing review of it in the *National Review*.[2] Directly overshadowing the spot where Henry Adams had lamented that American culture felt only the educational influence of the dynamo—the drive for more technological power, more energy—and none of the civilizing influence of devotion to the Virgin, the *sedes sapientiae* of the medieval universities, American Catholics raised the largest church in North America, the Shrine of the Immaculate Conception, at the heart of a pontifical university. These were the years when the Canadian spring waters of Etienne Gilson's influence spread from the Pontifical Institute of Medieval Studies in Toronto to the pontifical Catholic University of America and from thence in smaller but just as refreshing streams to every little Catholic college in America; the years when even Princeton and Columbia made a place for Jacques Maritain during his wartime exile; the years when Catholic priests marched arm-in-arm through the streets of Chicago with Martin Luther King, Jr., who—Methodist-educated at Boston University—appealed to Thomas Aquinas in his *Letter from a Birmingham Jail* to explain to America that "an unjust law is a human law that is not rooted in eternal law and natural law."

My copy of Christopher Dawson's *Crisis of Western Education* is a relic of that era when, together, neo-scholastics and neo-classicists discovered, in retrospect, an idea of the American university to defend against the specialization and technocracy that they thought might very well be the precursors of "a new dark age made more sinister, and perhaps more protracted, by the lights of perverted science" (the phrase is Winston Churchill's in his "Finest Hour" speech, June 18, 1940). Annotated in its margins, bearing the various-colored underlining that indicates multiple readings, it was clearly deemed worthy of being preserved in a private library. Yet, between the covers of the text, Dawson's "penetrating mind" remains self-consciously on the outskirts of American higher education. The thrust of Dawson's argument, as the *Commonweal* blurb summed it up, was that "it is now time for Christians to work for a *restoration* of Christian culture rather than to fight a merely defensive action in a purely *conservative* spirit" (emphasis mine). In other words, Dawson, acting the role he studied in his great master St. Augustine—the role of prophetic judge of the historic moment that is now, weighed Western culture in the balance and found that restoration rather than preservation was the order of the day. Christianity, he judged, was no longer at the center of Western history. Neither Christianity nor a Christian approach to education, he argued, were in a hegemonic position in America or in the West in 1960. The Christian church, the Christian people, had ceased, Dawson seemed to say, to be the center of Western cultural development. "Penetrating" as Dawson's mind was, it knew itself to be eccentric to the centers of power of American history and in the development of American higher education. And in this, Dawson was an accurate prophet. Professors at Catholic universities now speak of "the days when the neo-Thomist movement was at its height." The English Catholic Revival and American neo-Thomist revival have now become respectable minor sub-fields for British and American intellectual historians like myself (in what other department than history would you now be allowed to write a doctoral dissertation on G. K. Chesterton at a major, secular university?). The leaders of the movement and its classic authors have disappeared from major American Catholic universities' curricula, except where they hold on as one more of the many special programs, honors programs, institutes, and societies that cling like barnacles to the modern research university. Remnants have found refuge in a new wave of self-consciously eccentric Christian liberal arts colleges founded in the 1970s, eighties and nineties. And yet—and here arises the deeper paradox of Dawson's little book—"penetrating" as Dawson's mind was, it did not occur to him that it was precisely there—outside the center, outside the city, ostracized—that the greatest educators of his own tradition had found a very powerful magisterial chair.

Must we conclude from the historical trajectory of twentieth-century higher education that the Greatest Generation's idea of the American university was all just a great mistake? The over-heated dream of a small but vocal band of WASP reactionaries? The final toast to the old country before the Irish Americans succumbed to the American frontier's liberationist effects? Without a doubt, the fact that the vocal Catholic wing of the movement went out with such a post-Vatican II bang drew renewed attention of historians of higher education to ye olde story of secularization. And the fact that two of the best known recent works on this historic trend have come out of Notre Dame—James Burtchaell's *The Dying of the Light* and George Marsden's collection, *The Secularization of the Academy*—might seem to indicate the best vantage point from which to view the grand denouement.

At the end of the twentieth century even Christian historians of higher education are more willing to admit a narrative of secularization and the lamentable decline of church schools, than they were at the end of the nineteenth century when such secularization narratives were being triumphantly written in advance by the proponents of the process. While the colleges of the early republic were founded by churches, they quite quickly accepted state or community tax support. Despite formal disestablishment and even an outright and outspoken commitment to the "free church" ideal, an informal Protestant establishment existed that was only really disrupted by the arrival of large numbers of Irish Catholics. The nineteenth-century first wave of secularization in the historic Protestant colleges was to some extent caused by the presence of Catholics—the non-conformist churches were forced to choose between actual financial disestablishment and secularization and they chose secularization; the twentieth-century second wave was more shocking to everyone's sensibilities as it took place most visibly within precisely those Catholic institutions which had earlier picked up the flag of independence from where it lay.

No, the Greatest Generation was not mistaken in finding a deep and abiding consonance between American Civilization and the Christian Faith. Their only mistake was in allowing the American public to support them in this discovery. The only mistake they made was in forgetting that their independence— their eccentricity—was the most American thing about them. I mean here eccentricity in two interrelated senses, in the sense used by Remi Brague in his book *The Roman Way*, translated into English as *Eccentric Culture: A Theory of Western Civilization*, and also in the sense used by Henry Adams, in his great autobiographical memoir, *The Education of Henry Adams*. For Remi Brague eccentricity means finding a point of reference, a source of vitality outside of oneself; eccentric education in this sense is emulation of some standard or model taken to be both "other" and "classic." For Henry Adams eccentricity means flight from control by the center, standing at a critical distance and establishing a certain independence from the center of power, standing off even from one's own will to power as reasonable judge, tempering power to human purposes.

America remains an eccentric culture in Brague and Adams's meaning. The proliferation of independent schools and indeed the growing popularity of home-schooling is the most American feature in the panorama of education today; the continued attachment to classical liberal education and faith-based college curricula is the most distinctively American contribution to the varieties of higher education available today. Independence has always been the American Dream in education as in other things—the problem has always, quite simply, been how to fund it.

ECCENTRICITY AS THE ESSENCE OF THE WEST

In *Eccentric Culture*, Remi Brague argues that Europe's defining character is its Romanity, which he describes as a self-conscious acceptance of one's position as the student of some cultural tradition of which one is not the inventor. Brague says that it was characteristic of Roman culture to see itself as secondary, as heir to a great tradition—imported or inherited, not autochthonous or self-made. The image of Aeneas carrying his father and his household gods to his new homeland was central to the myth of Rome's cultural secondarity. Romanity is to accept one's position as eccentric to the center of culture, as Rome embraced its position as eccentric to the two cultural centers of Athens and Jerusalem. Rome accepted itself as a student and transmitter of Hellenism and Judeo-Christianity. Roads and aqueducts are Rome's greatest cultural symbols, Brague says—signs of its eagerness to pass on the civilized culture that they had inherited rather than created.

This European culture of *imitatio*, the Roman ethos of emulation of classic models, Brague argues, was consolidated during the Christian middle ages. Brague argues that the Christian faith came together with the Roman culture of secondarity, bringing its own inherent sense of secondarity with regard to the Jewish religious tradition. He argues that "Christianity . . . constitutes the very form of the European relationship to its cultural heritage. . . . The Christian model of the attitude toward the past, such as it is founded on the religious level in the secondarity of Christianity vis-à-vis the Old Covenant, structures the whole relationship."

Moreover, the essential element of the Jewish tradition, from which the Christian church has never wholly separated itself, Brague argues, is that movement by which "Judaism freed itself from the primitive connection . . . that associated each people to its respective god in such a way that the attachment to the god constituted a people as a political entity."[4] This idea of the separation of the temporal and spiritual, that the religious domain and the political domain are distinct, is consolidated by revelation via the Incarnate God, Jesus Christ—an event that proclaims with great absoluteness and finality that true religion is not humanity's highest philosophy, and that no right secular ordering is the cause of humanity's highest religious vision, which comes to it rather from outside history. Brague here suggests the interpenetration of Romanity and Christianity: "First, *the idea of incarnation forms a whole with religious secondarity*; second, *the idea of a separation of the temporal and the spiritual forms a whole with cultural secondarity.*"⁵

At the end of his essay, Brague asks whether Europe is still Roman, whether Europe is still eccentric in its fundamental cultural orientation, whether Europe is still Judeo-Christian, whether it still considers itself the bearer of a message that it received as a gift from some source outside itself, or whether it has collapsed into itself, into an egocentricity that will end in starvation, infertility, and finally death. He answers that modern Europe has indeed been diverted into an obsession with innovation which has destroyed its uniquely fruitful relation to the past and to nature. For Brague, the nineteenth-century Romantic movement's glorification of pure Hellenism and pure Christianity (extracted both from Jewish roots and Roman imitations) represents the final dissolution of Europe's Romanity. Twentieth-century Europe, Brague suggests, thus arrived at a new gnosticism—imagining that it had nothing to learn from the past or from nature, it felt no restraints—it envisioned itself as radically new and cut off from all traditional sources of culture, morality, law, political, social, economic institutions, or thought and came to consider the natural world is an unformed chaos awaiting the technological making of mankind—a new gnosticism that enabled the rise of the totalitarian regimes that combined the religious and the political in a heady mysticism of a new world order looking to bring about the end of history. Brague's prescription for Europe's recovery of its identity—if it wishes to remain anything more than "a little cape on the Asian continent" (Valery)—is that it "must become once again, the place of the separation of the temporal and the spiritual . . . each recognizing the legitimacy of the other in its proper domain."⁶

ECCENTRICITY AS THE ESSENCE OF AMERICA

This chapter does not propose to address Brague's assessment of the European cultural situation, nor can it enter fully into the question as to whether America Civilization is the apotheosis of European Civilization—the child preserving the old faith, the old virtue, and old liberty after the senility and insanity of the parent—or the vanguard of European dissolution. The question of whether Christopher Columbus launched American Civilization as a modern escapee from the European dark ages of medieval superstition or as a Christ-bearing dove is a debate with five hundred years of history. I will simply turn, as Americans have so often done when domestic debates become interminable, to some eccentric source, to some visiting authority from abroad—a Tocqueville, a Dickens, a Milosz, a Solzhenitsyn—to answer the question.

Benedict XVI, following in the clear footsteps of John Paul II, the apostle of hope, has spoken clearly and repeatedly about how eccentric American civilization looks when viewed from the center of Europe. In his wonderful essay, "The Spiritual Roots of Europe: Yesterday, Today, and Tomorrow," written while still Cardinal Ratzinger, he, like Brague, sees the essential characteristic of the West as the "duality of powers," the doctrine of the separation of the powers of the emperor and the pope, which he traces to Pope Gelasius I (492–96).[7] Towards the end of that essay, he admits that perhaps this essential characteristic of the West survives best in the United States:

> We have to acknowledge that the Catholic Church today represents the largest single religious community in the United States, while American Catholics have incorporated the traditions of the free church regarding the relationship between the Church and politics, believing that a Church that is separate from the state better guarantees the moral foundation of the country. . . . In this position we can rightly see a continuation, adapted to the times, of the model of Pope Gelasius described earlier.[8]

This brief but forceful statement is, on consideration, a rather stunning reaffirmation of the post-war sense of American Catholics, embodied in John Courtney Murray's *We Hold These Truths*, of the consonance between the Catholic faith and the American project. There is a briskness, a simplicity, a clarity to Ratzinger's summing up of the American fidelity to the eccentricity that is the inner dynamic of European Civilization that might give Americans pause.

One might imagine that the eagle eye of Cardinal Ratzinger had managed to flash into the heart of the American project, into the centerpiece of the United States Constitution, the supremacy clause. Ratzinger, a reader of Tocqueville, somehow discerned from afar the fact that the supremacy clause in the United States Constitution is contained between the two clauses repudiating any economic or religious utopianism that such a constitutional *novus ordo seclorum* might inspire—the clauses reaffirming the mundane duty of repaying all debts contracted prior to the adoption of the new constitution and clarifying that while an oath of loyalty to the constitution would be required of all officers of the new government, "no religious test shall ever be required as a qualification to any office or public trust under the United States." The supremacy clause thus answered rather precisely the demand for a new constitution made by George Washington in his 1783 Letter to the States—a letter which scolds the states for refusing to acknowledge any "debts of honor" contracted during the war for independence, debts to those who had offered "their lives, their fortunes, and their sacred honor" to the cause of liberty.

Washington's famous letter demanding a constitutional convention at the moment that the peace treaty was signed was a statement very typical of the man who would be dubbed by eulogists throughout the land the American Aeneas (that great bearer of eccentric gods to new lands) and the American Moses (that great resistor of Pharaoh, his chariots and charioteers)—a clear statement of the very idea of "constitutionalism," that political sovereignty is always limited by a law that stands below and above it, the laws of nature and nature's God, the rights with which all men are created.[9] Washington's affirmation of the existence of "duties of honor" was an affirmation of this notion of constitutionalism, a demand for some acknowledgment of a law eccentric to the mere will of the majority. This commitment to the rule of law eccentric to the rule of the majority has a strangely central place in the American tradition—from Lincoln's affirmation in his Peoria Address that even if one were to "repeal all [political] compromises—repeal the dec- laration of independence—repeal all past history—you still cannot repeal human nature" to Martin Luther King's "an unjust law is a human law that is not rooted in eternal law and natural law." Perhaps this fundamental, constitutional American commitment to eccentricity has been obscured by particular laws, particular interpretations of the constitution, and particular interpretations of America history as taught in public schools; it is thus, all the more interesting that it remains visibly and distinctively American to a visitor from abroad.

On his visit to the United States in 2008, Benedict XVI celebrated this same eccentricity in American history with particular regard to education. In his address at the Catholic University of America, he reminded Catholic educators that "the history of this nation includes many examples" of the church's leading role in education. He celebrated the vitality of independent, church-based educational initiatives, which have contributed so much to the vitality of the moral discourse in the public forum. He applauded the Catholic community's willingness to accept the burden of education as "integral to the mission of the Church to proclaim the Good News" even to the point of "great sacrifice." He noted in particular the "remarkable network of parochial schools" and the committed efforts towards "educating those whom others had neglected." He also showed a clear awareness that "some today ques- tion the Church's involvement in education," that "at times the value of the Church's contribution to the public forum is questioned." Against those who would separate education from the evangelical mission of the Church, he insisted that it is precisely by affirming the independence and distinctiveness of the Church's role in education—which "stems from her awareness that she is the bearer of a message which has its origin in God himself"—that Christian educational institutions can play a role which is "consonant with a nation's fundamental aspiration to develop a society truly worthy of the human person's dignity."

CHALLENGING THE SECULARIZATION OF THE AMERICAN ACADEMY MASTER-NARRATIVE

If Remi Brague is correct in saying that it is the Judeo-Christian faith in a transcendent God, not only separate from the life of a particular tribe or political community but outside human history, that ultimately grounds the classical culture of emulation; and if Benedict XVI is correct in discerning that, at least in comparison with Europe, America remains a profoundly Christian nation with a strong tradition of independent, church-supported liberal education; what are we to make of the mainlines of the history of American higher education? That story as it has been told for two hundred years, whether in celebration or in lamentation, has been the story of unremitting secularization.

Even Henry Adams's *Education*, his great memoir-style protest against the secularization of the American university in his life-time and thus the loss of the very character of university—despite being a protest—seemed only to further establish the main storyline of the field. "If Harvard or Yale had been less foolish in their origins and had held onto the Church, we should have probably kept a base on which to build some real scholarship; but when our ancestors cut off the limb that made us a part of the tree, we naturally tumbled off. I do not suppose we ever produced a graduate who would have known how to sacrifice a bull to Jupiter."[10] He argues that powerful as the literary and political tradition was in America, in the Boston of his youth, at Harvard, it was devoid of any religious underpinnings:

> Of all the conditions of his youth which afterwards puzzled the grown-up man, this disappearance of religion puzzled him most. The boy went to church twice every Sunday; he was taught to read his Bible, and he learned religious poetry by heart; he believed in a mild deism; he prayed; he went through all the forms; but neither to him nor to his brothers or sisters was religion real. Even the mild discipline of the Unitarian Church was so irksome that they all threw it off at the first possible moment, and never afterwards entered a church. The religious instinct had vanished, and could not be revived, although one made in later life many efforts to recover it. That the most powerful emotion of man, next to the sexual, should disappear, might be a personal defect of his own; but that the most intelligent society, led by the most intelligent clergy, in the most moral conditions he ever knew, should have solved all the problems of the universe so thoroughly as to have quite ceased making itself anxious about past or future,

and should have persuaded itself that all the problems which had convulsed human thought from earliest recorded time, were not worth discussing, seemed to him the most curious social phenomenon he had to account for in a long life.

His memoir of his later years, after his wife's suicide, and the insanity and death of his close friend Clarence King who he had once thought represented the perfection of the frontier American, becomes an agonized, strained search for faith—he spends his final years touring the French countryside in his new motor car, trying to catch some whiff of faith from the power of the Virgin, which he acknowledges still retains its force at Lourdes.

But his own failure and the triumph of secularization was never Henry Adams' point—rather, as he argues repeatedly, "eccentricity is strength," and American history, like human history, gives up its prophetic ghost to those who are willing to read it in silence, to those who will listen rather than forever reciting their own variety of pseudo-religious experiences. Adams is a believer. He believes that Americans who flew into the wilderness in 1620, in 1776, in 1845, in 1892—who knew that the only way to save their nation was to leave it behind—carrying their household gods on their backs, have not been defeated. Henry Adams realized that the restraints of a fixed religious, cultural, familial, or political tradition were only superficially a "handicap." He repeatedly compared himself, "American of Americans, with Heaven knew how many Puritans and Patriots behind him and an education that had cost a civil war," with a sort of pride and arrogant relish, to a "Polish Jew fresh from Warsaw or Cracow . . . a furtive Yacoob or Ysaac still reeking of the ghetto, snarling in weird Yiddish." In the "races of the twentieth-century," the race to abandon all restraints of past or nature, to strip oneself of all prejudicial identity and submit oneself, the naked servant and worshipper of the dynamo, he asserted (strangely enough!) that the American cultural tradition would prove as resistant to the worship of the twentieth-century Alexanders, Pharaohs, and Caesars, as the Jewish cultural tradition had ever proven. It is a breath-taking claim—the claim that American eccentricity can survive 600-pages worth of experiential learning and never lose its old illusions about liberty, virtue, or wisdom!

What then are we to make of this narrative of the liberationist effects of the American frontier on the old-world traditions imported from Europe; what are we to make of the story of the tabula rasa, the erasure, the secularization, the oblivion of the past and its lessons, prejudices and constraints? Henry Adams's assertion invites us to look again at the meaning of the history of American higher education:

Harvard was founded to help the Puritans escape Anglican Oxford and Cambridge, and Yale appeared in 1701 when a group of New Haven ministers, influenced in part by distrust of the liberal heresies that were to dominate Harvard, established a competing college to preserve the old social and religious order in Connecticut. Again, the Congregationalists who founded Amherst were in part moved by the objections to the Unitarianism that shook Harvard in the early 19th century, and the Yankee Methodists who set up Boston University at the time of the Civil War felt that Harvard's classical curriculum and aristocratic values were destroying the ethos of pious dissent. The same era also saw the Jesuits establish Boston College, to help the new Boston-Irish community maintain its religious and social integrity. (Riesman in Sanford, 89)

From this history can we say that it is secularization or the perennial escape to eccentric orthodoxy that is the core "American" dynamic of the history higher education in this country? Is the declension of Harvard from Puritan seminary to Unitarian classical college to secular multiversity the inner dynamic of American higher education, or has the original eccentric dynamic of Harvard's Christian orthodoxy simply metastasized in hundreds of small Bible colleges and Christian liberal arts colleges across the country? Are not these small Christian liberal arts colleges the truly American—the most distinctively American—contribution to the idea of the university in the modern world?[11] Whatever one thinks of such quaint neo-medieval, neo-classical flora and fauna sprouting in the American frontier—whether one considers them the hope for the future of Western Civilization or embarrassing windows into the reactionary mind of middle America, it can hardly be denied that they, and not the anonymous, mega-state-universities of the great cities, are the peculiarly American features of the modern educational landscape.

Alasdair MacIntyre, in the now famous final paragraph of his work *After Virtue*, prescribed another round of that excellent habit of running away:

It is always dangerous to draw too precise parallels between one historical period and another; and among the most misleading of such parallels are those which have been drawn between our own age in Europe and North America and the epoch in which the Roman empire declined into the Dark Ages. Nonetheless certain parallels there are. A crucial turning point in that earlier history occurred when men and women of good will turned aside from the task of shoring up the Roman *imperium* and ceased to identify the continuation of civility and moral community with the maintenance of that *imperium*. What they set themselves to achieve instead—often not realizing what fully what they were doing—was the construction of new forms of community within which the moral life could be sustained so that both morality and civility might survive the coming ages of barbarism and darkness. If my account of our moral condition is correct, we ought also to conclude that for some time now we too have reached that turning point. What matters at this stage is the construction of local forms of community within which civility and the intellectual and moral life can be sustained through the new dark ages which are already upon us. And if the tradition of the virtues was able to survive the horrors of the last dark ages, we are not entirely without grounds for hope. This time, however, the barbarians are not waiting beyond the frontiers; they have already been governing us for quite some time. And it is our lack of consciousness of this that constitutes part of our predicament. We are waiting not for a Godot, but for another—doubtless quite different—St. Benedict.

'Tis sure to be an immortal paragraph. But (dare I say that) Alasdair MacIntyre, like Christopher Dawson, indeed like Edward Gibbon, imagines that this "construction of local forms of community within which civility and the intellectual and moral life can be sustained" is a "turning aside from the task of shoring up the Roman Imperium." Yet these Britishers never fully grasp that this English, Scottish, Irish, Jewish, Polish, Italian habit of running away with their traditions on their backs is actual *pietas* to the founders of the imperium. Eccentricity is a very American virtue.

Indeed George Washington himself knew the value of a strategic retreat that might keep one's ragtag army intact—to fight another day . . . or at any rate to hold out until one can find an ally with a navy.[12]

NOTES

1. From St. Mary's College website: "The Christian Culture Lecture was founded in 1957 by Saint Mary's professor Bruno Schlesinger, PhD, who also introduced Christian Culture as a major at the College in 1956. The major was later renamed Humanistic Studies. At its inception the lecture series was largely funded through a grant from the Lilly Foundation. By 1981, the series had become increasingly difficult to administer and it fell silent for 25 years. Through the generosity of Susan Fitzgerald Rice '61, a Christian Culture major, and her husband Donald B. Rice, the Christian Culture Lecture was resurrected in 2006. The Christian Culture Lecture features a distinguished humanities scholar who explores some aspect of the Christian dimension of Western culture." "Humanistic Studies examines the literature, history, and art of western culture as an integrated whole, from the end of the Roman Empire to the present. Founded as the Christian Culture Program in 1956, it features a 'great books' program and pays special attention to the role played by Christianity, by women, and by non-western cultures in the making of western civilization."

2. William F. Buckley, *National Review*, January 28, 1961, began, "John Courtney Murray, SJ, is one of those glamorous people you are always hearing about, and are left wanting to hear more. He is a dashing man, and an intimate of those among the high and mighty who are lucky enough to engross him—and how hard a job that must be! Once he told a reporter from the *New York Post* that Henry Luce tends to talk too much after dinner (theirs is a non-confessional relationship). He spends occasional

weekends in East Hampton; and when he is the guest of honor, the list is screened with special care. He was appointed visiting lecturer at Yale University for one year in 1951. Through his stay he gave three public lectures. To everyone's astonishment, he filled the large Law School Auditorium to overflowing—an unheard-of feat for a resident scholar, let alone a minister of God."

3. Remi Brague, *Eccentric Culture: A Theory of Western Civilization*, 176.

4. Brague, *Eccentric Culture*, 157.

5. Brague, *Eccentric Culture*, 163.

6. Brague, *Eccentric Culture*, 189.

7. Cardinal Joseph Ratzinger, "The Spiritual Roots of Europe: Yesterday, Today, and Tomorrow," 56–57.

8. Ratzinger, "The Spiritual Root of Europe," 71.

9. Herman Belz, "Written Constitutionalism as the American Project," and "Constitutionalism and the American Founding," in *A Living Constitution or Fundamental Law? American Constitutionalism in Historical Perspective* (Lanham: Rowman and Littlefield, 1998); Robert P. Hay, "George Washington: American Moses," *American Quarterly* 21, no. 4 (Winter 1969), 780–91; John C. Shields, *The American Aeneas: Classical Origins of the American Self (Knoxville: University of Tennessee Press, 2001).*

10. *The Letters of Henry Adams*, Volume VI: 1906–1918, ed. J. C. Leverson, Ernest Samuels, Charles Vandersee, Viola Hopkins Winner (Cambridge, Mass.: The Belknap Press of Harvard University Press, 1988), Massachusetts Historical Society, Volume VI: 419, To Frederick Bliss Luquiens.

11. Most of the writing on higher education in America by Christians and conservatives has the character of a lament. But what needs to be affirmed is that the struggle for survival and fidelity of schools dedicated to Christian faith and the dignity of the human person is natural to a fallen world, and nothing is peculiarly wrong with either the American idea of the university or American society and culture because the Christian liberal arts college is difficult to maintain in practice.

12. Not all unhelped we held the fort, our tiny flags unfurled;
Some giants laboured in that cloud to lift it from the world.
I find again the book we found, I feel the hour that flings
Far out of fish-shaped Paumanok some cry of cleaner things;
And the Green Carnation withered, as in forest fires that pass,
Roared in the wind of all the world ten million leaves of grass;
Or sane and sweet and sudden as a bird sings in the rain—
Truth out of Tusitala spoke and pleasure out of pain.
Yea, cool and clear and sudden as a bird sings in the grey,
Dunedin to Samoa spoke, and darkness unto day.
But we were young; we lived to see God break their bitter charms.
God and the good Republic come riding back in arms:
We have seen the City of Mansoul, even as it rocked, relieved—
Blessed are they who did not see, but being blind, believed. (G. K. Chesterton)

II

Higher Education and Democracy

6

Socrates in America

William Mathie

In the seventh book of Plato's *Republic,* Socrates proposes "an image of our nature in its education and its want of education" (514a).[1] Socrates asks Glaucon, his young interlocutor, to imagine human beings prisoners in a cave bound so that they can see neither themselves nor their fellows. Behind these prisoners and above them is a fire; that fire is the only source of light in this cave. Between fire and prisoners is a low wall. Other human beings who carry artifacts and statues of men and other animals above them pass behind this wall casting shadows on the wall in front of the prisoners. Socrates' imagined prisoners seem strange to Glaucon, and they may well seem strange to us. But Socrates says the prisoners are "like us." They are "like us" in the first place by virtue of the fact that "they have seen nothing of themselves or one another *except for the shadows* cast by the fire upon the side of the cave they face" (515a). As for the things carried mysteriously along the wall behind them, if the prisoners should enter into dialogue with one another, they would suppose that when they name the shadows of those things in front of them they are naming things that are, and are as they seem. If the cave also has an echo such that the occasional sounds of the human beings moving along behind the wall bounce off the cave side facing them, the prisoners will suppose that it is the shadows that are making those sounds.

Socrates then describes a prisoner who happens "by nature" to be released from his bonds, who is forced to turn toward the fire and the objects whose shadows he had previously observed, and who is interrogated about these objects and told that he is now "closer to what is" and "turned towards beings." This freed prisoner, Socrates says, would believe the shadows of his former world "truer" than these new things. He would resist if forced to look towards the fire, and he would be pained if dragged by force up and out of the cave. Blinded at first by the glare of daylight as he leaves the cave, Socrates goes on to describe how his escaped prisoner would proceed in the world outside the cave. He would look first upon the shadows and reflections of things, then upon the things themselves, next upon the stars and moon in the night sky, and finally upon the sun itself. And, according to Socrates, he would somehow be able to identify the sun as the source of seasons and years, ruler of all visible things, and cause of all that he has seen. Finally, Socrates imagines his prisoner returned to his former place in the cave. Again he would be blinded—this time his eyes must adjust from light to darkness—and he is as a result unable to compete with his fellow prisoners in the game they play of remembering the order of the shadows on the wall of the cave. His fellow prisoners would say that he had been corrupted. If they could get their hands on whoever freed him and dragged him out of the cave they would kill him.

Socrates says that this is an image of our education. I suppose we can say that he is describing liberal education, and there is a long tradition that suggests Socrates is exactly the person to whom we must turn if we would understand what liberal education is. Yet there is much that is perplexing about Socrates' image of liberal education. Not least is the fact that so many of us—even those who like little else in the *Republic*—are pleased by this image. Do we not show by our pleasure that we count ourselves among the class of the escaped prisoners? But when did we suffer the pain Socrates associates with turning from the shadows to the firelight that caused those shadows, or with ascending from the cave, or with preparing to gaze upon the sun?

A second puzzle is this: how does Socrates know what the image seems to tell us? Has he been out of the cave? Has he seen the sun? How can we reconcile his image here with his claim, in the *Apology*, that his only wisdom is his awareness of his ignorance? Or does knowing that we do not know *mean* knowing that it is a cave we inhabit? In any case, if are out of the cave, how did we escape? How could anyone *ever* get out of the cave, if we take seriously Socrates' account of how we are imprisoned there? Indeed, does Socrates mean to suggest that escape through our own efforts is impossible when he introduces a mysterious liberator who employs force to free his prisoners from their bonds, turn them towards the light, and drag them out of the cave (515e–516a)? But if we need a teacher-liberator, how was our liberator liberated? Who was our teacher's teacher?

I am a teacher of political science in a Canadian publicly funded university that has recently abandoned its once real though always fragile commitment to something like liberal education. I am confident that many of the things

I see in my own university are duplicated in many other secular institutions of post-secondary education throughout North America. I have in mind the collusion of administrators and permanent faculty in substituting research of uncertain intellectual significance for teaching so that permanent faculty are less and less in the classroom, and the "delivery" of most of our programs to most of our students is through ill-paid and not always well qualified temporary instructors. Where I teach we call this becoming a "comprehensive university." I have in mind also the unionization of permanent faculty and of temporary instructors, which has turned most serious pedagogical and curricular questions into management-employee issues of workload—at the long and short-run expense of our students. I have in mind the agreement of our government, university administrators and faculty to the idea of what we call "accessibility," which means, first, that no one should be kept out of university for almost any reason, and, secondly, that we are morally bound by our initial agreement to those we admit to make it feasible for all of them to get what they came for: a degree. And I have in mind the version of the tyranny of political correctness from which we suffer and our promotion of which we call—without conscious irony—diversity. Many might have heard of the recent experiment at one of Canada's most distinguished universities (Queen's) to employ under-cover "tolerance police" who would be on the alert for unsuitable conversations on campus, and who would enter into those conversations so as to redirect them along more appropriate lines.

Clearly these are great threats to the very possibility of liberal education in the university, and we must resist them however and whenever we can. What I know of these things is known to many who are familiar with higher education, but if they are threats to almost any defensible *idea of the university*, their exploration can only indirectly help us see what that idea might be.

My reflections occasioned by the title of this volume are not all dark. They include thinking about that handful of extraordinary students who still appear from time to time full of that longing for what liberal education offers, and whose scarcity Allan Bloom had in mind when he gave *The Closing of the American Mind* its original title: *souls without longing*. And I am led to recall my own good luck in encountering two wonderful teachers—both of them, as it happens, political philosophers—and in discovering indirectly, through my fellow graduate students at the University of Chicago, the Great Books Program of St. John's College. My own reflections upon the subject of liberal education have amounted to a life-long effort to think together what I learned about learning from those two teachers—one a Canadian, George Grant, and the other a refugee from Hitler's Germany, Leo Strauss—and what I learned by trying to pursue the aims and methods of the Great Books program in my own classes and in the great books program we established some twenty years ago at my university.

"Socrates was a great and good man. Democracy is a good thing. Socrates must be a democrat." So runs the popular fallacy we encounter so often inside and outside our classrooms. The same fallacy might enter into the thoughts even of those who read a book like this one. All of us are friends of liberal education, whether or not we are employed in the providing of it, and indeed many or most of our colleagues in academia and our fellow citizens are also well disposed toward liberal education, except to the extent that those more closely connected with the paying of the bills—whether the parents of students or governments—sometimes fret that liberal education is very expensive and might not train people especially well in the skills that enable them to pay, or repay, those bills.

And most of us are democrats: We are immediately suspicious of inequalities, especially inequalities that are big and enduring. Mostly, popularity is a compelling argument for anything or anyone. In any case, all of us are forced to make our arguments in the language (or languages) of democracy. Opponents and critics of quota systems for admission or hiring both claim to be advancing equality. We are inclined to suppose then that if liberal education and liberal democracy are both good things, each must somehow be good for the other. So far as we must defend our programs and institutions before our fellow citizens or elected representatives of the democracy, we are forced to justify liberal education as something that contributes to liberal democracy—maybe even as something necessary to democracy.

But are liberal education and democracy entirely harmonious? One could say that democracy depends more than any other regime does upon education, just because it is rule of the many by the many, and therefore self-rule of a kind. But this statement is open to the objection that it applies, if at all, only to some long deceased ancient version of democracy, and even then to what was at best a democracy of a small number of male citizens whose freedom depended upon the political exclusion of women and slavery. Modern democracy might rather be described—is often described—as the rule of a bureaucracy under elites who compete for political power by occasional appeals for the electoral approval of the mass. Modern democracy is rule by competing elites within a mass culture. Leo Strauss once wrote that "liberal education is the ladder by which we try to ascend from mass democracy to democracy as originally meant. Liberal education is the necessary endeavor to found an aristocracy within democratic mass culture."[2] In fact, very few of the things we study in pursuing what is usually described as a liberal education—the books we read, the paintings we admire, the music we listen to—originated in democratic societies, and most of them do not exactly fit within the assumptions of democracy. It should be enough to think of the greatest hero of our greatest poem, Achilles in Homer's *Iliad*, or to recall what Socrates says, in Plato's *Crito* about how little regard we should have for the opinion of the many, who would put to death someone at one moment, and at the next want to raise him up again. And many even of the works we study in the course of a liberal education that *were* conceived within a liberal democracy are far more hostile to that regime than contemporary critics of the canon commonly notice.

My aim in this chapter is to explore the relationship between liberal education and liberal democracy by considering the implicit account of that relationship we find in Tocqueville's *Democracy in America,* and especially in his discussion of how democracy affects the movement of the intellect in the United States (429, [401]).[3] Why Tocqueville? First, I note that this is just where Allan Bloom began his justly famous account of the university in America: "Tocqueville taught me the importance of the university to democracy," Bloom wrote.[4] And if liberal education is, as Strauss wrote, "the necessary endeavor to found an aristocracy within democratic mass society," Tocqueville seems the best possible guide for that endeavor. If *Democracy in America* is, or contains, the new science of politics that Tocqueville says we need in order to educate the newly emerging democracy of modernity, we cannot help noting that the analysis of democracy his book contains shows what democracy is by constantly comparing it to the aristocracy it is replacing. If, as I mean to suggest, Tocqueville's book does *not* finally reveal the right *idea of the American university,* seeing why this is so may be a good first step in looking for that idea.

Suppose, then, we ask ourselves whether democracy favors liberal education, and pose this question within the understanding of democracy that Tocqueville provides. Suppose we ask, in other words, whether it is democracy—or aristocracy—that is more inclined to promote liberal education or its ends? We might be inclined at first to argue the case for democracy when we reflect that democracy seems on Tocqueville's account to be far closer to the truth than its fundamental alternative, aristocracy, in several ways. The code of honor in an aristocracy is, for example, often made up of what at first glance seem bizarre rules—rules that become explicable only when one sees that they maintained the position and power of some small body within the larger society. Indeed, in honoring "the virtues that have greatness and luster and that can be readily combined with pride and love of power . . . [the aristocratic honor code] is not afraid to disturb the natural order of conscience" (587, [591]). In a democracy the rules of honor become simpler, much less rigorous, and less strange as they increasingly coincide with what Tocqueville calls the permanent interests and natural needs of mankind. Members of an aristocratic society who are divided from one another by "property, profession, and birth" barely think of themselves as "forming part of the same humanity" (538, [535]). Thus even the wisest of the ancients never "managed to grasp at this idea so general but at the same time so simple as the likeness of all men and of the equal right to freedom that each of them acquires at birth; [instead] they took pains to prove that slavery was natural and that it would exist always" (437, [413]). Indeed, according to Tocqueville, aristocracy is at its core founded upon and maintained by an illusion. The fundamental law of aristocracy is a rule of inheritance that maintains the great holdings of property in land that are the basis of the power of the rulers of that society. What causes men and societies to adhere to a system of primogeniture which is contrary to the true self-interest of even the wealthy is the "illusion" that one can achieve immortality through one's family. When the aristocratic laws of inheritance are abolished, Tocqueville says "individual egoism returns to its true inclinations" (78, [49]). Democracy is moreover closely linked to the Cartesian insistence upon judging everything for oneself. In aristocracy, on the other hand, our opinions are most often those of our class or our ancestors. Nor is this so only among the powerful and wealthy in aristocratic society. Tocqueville asks us to think of the servant who so completely identifies with the welfare and privileged status of his master as to obliterate himself: "the servant ends by losing his sense of self-interest; he becomes detached from it; he deserts himself as it were, or rather he transports the whole of himself into his master; he there creates an *imaginary* personality for himself" (551, [549], emphasis added).

In these and other respects, we might be led to say that democracy is closer to the truth about human nature and less dependent upon illusion, and so is the natural home of liberal education. If liberal education holds with Socrates that the unexamined life is not worth living, that examination must surely be favored by the destruction of the arbitrary inequalities and illusions that characterize aristocracy.

Upon further reflection, however, we are forced to admit that a society that accords with the truth about human nature and does away with all illusions might not be a society that favors the pursuit of the truth. We remember, for example, that the first city founded by Socrates in Plato's *Republic*, based on the simplest economic needs is a city Socrates calls "true" or "truthful," but his interlocutor, the young and noble Glaucon, scorns as "a city of pigs." And whatever we think about that city, we know that it lacked both philosophy and poetry, as well as politics. In any case, there are strong reasons for doubting whether democracy as it is understood by Tocqueville is the home of liberal education. Consider again what looks like about the strongest point in democracy's favor—that it favors judging everything for oneself. In fact, this principle of judging everything for oneself turns out to be at best ambiguous, according to Tocqueville's analysis. In the first place, Tocqueville points out, we can never judge everything for ourselves, as the Cartesian principle seems to demand—societies and individuals and even philosophers need to take many or most things for granted. They need what Tocqueville calls dogmatic opinions, and those opinions must come from somewhere. In democracy we get the dogmatic opinions we need from public opinion as it is constituted by the majority. In fact, public opinion in democracy is a more pervasive power than any we find in any other kind of society. The denial of the very possibility of intellectual superiority which defines democratic society and establishes the Cartesian principle, in truth shuts each of us up inside ourselves in such a way as to make inaccessible any notion of truth or beauty. To understand this we need to look more closely at how exactly the equality of social conditions that defines democracy leads to the principle of judging for oneself. When human beings live in a society subject to what appear to them great and permanent divisions, they do not see how much other members of their species actually resemble them. They are willing to acknowledge that other human beings may be wiser than they are: They accept in principle the idea of intellectual authority—what Tocqueville calls the "idea of the superior." But as human beings become more equal and alike (*semblable*), this idea— the willingness to admit the possibility that some other human being might be our intellectual superior—collapses. This is not to say that what we see when permanent unequal divisions disappear is the truth, that all human beings are truly alike and equal. According to Tocqueville they are not. Rather he says more precisely that what happens when aristocracy is gone is not something we see but something we do not see—we see no signs of incontestable superiority. One could say that in aristocratic society the idea of the superior was based upon ignorance—human beings could imagine others to be their superiors because those others were not seen up close.[5] But one must add that what replaces the aristocratic ignorance that is open to the idea of the superior is an ignorance that denies the very possibility of excellence or wisdom. And what takes the place of the wisdom of some particular others, of one's ancestors or one's superiors, is unlimited dependence upon public opinion.

A similar impasse confronts us when we ask whether liberal education serves democracy, whether democracy somehow needs or depends upon liberal education, again posing our question within the understanding of democracy provided by Tocqueville. In the first place, we might recall that though the equality of social conditions, which above all defines democracy for Tocqueville, is certain—a matter of fate or providence—freedom in liberal democracy is much less certain; a soft but enervating democratic despotism is at least as likely an expression of that equality as is political freedom. Though perfect equality can only be achieved where there is also perfect liberty, much of what the passion for equality wants can be obtained without liberty, and sometimes even at its expense. Though the desire for equality can be the ennobling desire to bring others up to our level, it is far more often expressed in the desire to bring others down to our level. And the passion for equality in modern times is far more powerful than the love of liberty (494, [480]). Considering the fragility of liberty in democracy, we might readily imagine that liberal education could furnish an invaluable antidote to the enervation of the human soul with which democracy threatens us. On further investigation, however, we see that what Tocqueville identifies as the greatest preserver of the democratic republic is not liberal education but something quite different and almost contrary to it.

Tocqueville says that what has chiefly preserved democratic freedom in America—more than her laws or constitutional order and more than her physical circumstances—is American mores (*les moeurs* or morals and manners). And what this chiefly means for Tocqueville is American religion. Tocqueville's European readers who think the persistence of religion in America a remnant of the past that will eventually disappear as democracy advances are badly mistaken. Religion has not been the foe of democracy in America as it has been in Europe, where it had allied itself with the political forces opposed to democracy. In fact, religion has carefully removed itself from any direct role in political life in America. Rather than seek political help religion has relied entirely upon the support that comes to it out of its natural place in human life as a hope that answers to the human anxiety that arises out of our awareness of our mortality.

How does religion contribute to the preservation of liberty in American democracy? It limits or redirects the "individualism" that threatens to confine democratic man "in the solitude of his own heart" (497, [484]) by the application of the "doctrine of self-interest rightly understood" to "religious beliefs" (514, [504]).[6] By preserving some notion of the human soul as distinct from the body, religion limits the excesses to which the taste for material enjoyments peculiar to democracy may go. Indeed, Tocqueville adds that oblivion of the soul even undermines the peculiarly human manner of pursuing the goods of the body.[7] Finally, it is religion above all that stands in the way of the terrible tyranny possible within democracy.

Religion entails at least some limit to the possible presumption of majority opinion that it can do anything. Religion sets this limit by furnishing an answer to each of what Tocqueville calls the "primordial" questions about God, the soul, and our relations to God and other human beings. The answers religion furnishes to these questions Tocqueville describes as "clear, precise, intelligible to the crowd and very durable" (441, [418]). He also calls them "firm ideas (idées bien arrêtées)" and says "men have a huge interest in making for themselves firm ideas" about these things. Why exactly is this so important for Tocqueville? We see his answer in his description of what happens to a people in whom religion is destroyed:

> Doubt impairs the highest elements of the intellect and partly paralyses all the others. Each becomes accustomed to having only confused and changing notions about matters that most interest those like oneself and oneself . . . and as one despairs of being able to resolve for oneself [these] great problems, one is reduced, like a coward, to not thinking about them at all.
>
> Such a state cannot fail to enervate souls; it slackens the springs of the will and prepares citizens for servitude.

Religion is, we might say, just one more of those dogmas made necessary in light of the incapacity of individuals and societies to judge all things for themselves. But it is of critical importance, as we can see by considering what happens when it is absent. It is, Tocqueville says, "the matter about which it is most important that each of us have fixed ideas; and unfortunately it is also the one in which it is most difficult [for the ordinary person], left to himself, and by the effort of his reason to come to fix his ideas." But is it possible for *anyone*, however free they might be of "the ordinary preoccupations of life," to "break through to these so necessary truths"? In fact, even those philosophers with the leisure and qualifications for this task "have been able to discover only a small number of contradictory notions, in the midst of which the human mind has constantly floated for thousands of years without being able to grasp firmly the truth" (441, [417]).

What exactly and how great then is the difference between a people in whom religion has been destroyed and one in which this is not the case? The difference would seem to correspond, I think, to that between what Tocqueville describes as "what ought to be, in our day, *the natural state* of men in the matter of religion" and what he found in America, and the alternative to that state in Europe that he laments. In the first case, the happy case of America, believers and non-believers enjoy a mutual good will, or at least sympathy, for each other. The believer pities the non-believers who have lost that dearest hope religious belief brings—he sees them as unfortunates, not adversaries. The unbeliever, for his part, regrets his own loss of belief and continues to view religion as useful; he has no wish to take their beliefs from others. In Europe, Tocqueville observes the contrary to the "natural state of men in the matter of religion." The scene is much less happy or peaceful. The adversaries of religion are ardent, while believers are mostly tepid—they hardly dare profess their belief—but a few of the faithful are "ready to brave all obstacles and scorn all dangers for their beliefs" and look upon the unbelievers with hatred.

What does Tocqueville mean by characterizing what he sees in America as the "natural state of men in the matter of religion"—and by adding "in our day"? Faith is natural to human beings, the result of "man's natural disgust for existence and his immense desire to exist" or of the human desire for immortality. But "in our day" that natural hope that seeks its satisfaction in religious belief must maintain itself after the powerful operation upon it of secret doctrines that have undermined existing religious beliefs without furnishing anything else in their place. One would have to penetrate to the souls of the Americans to discover the wounds religious faith has received in consequence of these prodigious revolutions working on the human mind "without the apparent aid of man's passions and so to speak without him suspecting them" (282, [286]). Religion is pervasive in Tocqueville's America and it is of critical importance in averting the dangers of democracy, but its apparent strength is misleading. The goodwill of believers and unbelievers in American democracy seems to be founded on the same implicit understanding on the part of each, that a critical examination of the claims of religious belief such as might result from believers defending the truth of their beliefs—or non-believers attacking those beliefs—would lead to their abandonment. But if this is correct, how far is the "natural state of men in the matter of religion"—the situation of religious belief in American democracy— from the cowardly reluctance to think about these questions that Tocqueville attributed to a people whose religion has been destroyed?

If democratic liberty is preserved by a religious faith that is itself maintained only because neither those who have it, nor those who have lost it, want to defend or question its truth, can we say that liberal education as it might be experienced by the American student or citizen who looks at his society in light of Tocqueville's critique might still belong to that effort "to found an aristocracy within democratic mass culture" that Strauss spoke of? The difficulty here is that the critique of liberal democracy constituted by liberal education, which we might gather out of Tocqueville's account of intellectual life and the arts in American democracy as it appeals to what is found within aristocracy, leads us to despise the way of life that is democracy. Consider Tocqueville's account of the "gravity of the Americans" as illustrated by the favorite recreation of the American—getting drunk in his own home (579, [582]). Or consider his account of why American men are so rarely guilty of adultery—lack of time, energy, and above all imagination (570, [571]). Despising the mores of democracy might be the beginning of a liberal education. It depends upon where we are left by that "despising." Recalling Tocqueville's insistence that aristocracy can never be re-established, that we must rather develop a new science of politics to overcome the dangers and secure the benefits that belong to democracy, we are forced to consider the moral and political consequences of a teaching that leads us to see at once the damage to the soul brought about in and by democracy and the impossibility of any political regime favorable to healthy souls.

What Tocqueville's analysis of democracy seems to show is the impossibility of that effort to "found an aristocracy within democratic mass culture" Strauss calls liberal education. Indeed, we can say of Tocqueville's picture of American democracy something very like what we said of Socrates' image of the cave. We are charmed by both, and yet on Tocqueville's own account of the omnipotence of public opinion in democracy it must be deeply mysterious that this charm should work upon us. But there is also this great difference between the situation in which we are left by the Socratic image and by Tocqueville's account of the democratic mind. If we may ask how Socrates can know that there is a world outside the cave, we are at least invited to imagine that world, and somehow to associate it with Socrates and the Socratic way of life—the life of philosophy. Tocqueville's unveiling of democracy is not one that leads us to imagine a world outside, or above, the world of democracy. To be sure, we see the grim features of democracy as they are contrasted to the more attractive, even beautiful hues of aristocracy, but we know that the world of aristocracy is irretrievably past, *and* we know that the beauties of that world were founded on illusions. And we know that the religious faith that prevents the worst dangers and excesses of democracy is maintained by wilfully blind hope—a hope that dare not risk an argument with anyone who might question it. Do we find in Tocqueville's account of democracy an understanding of things in the light of which liberal education might perform the task for democracy Strauss has described? If not, where might we turn for such an understanding?

The title of this volume recalls, of course, what is probably the most famous of all arguments for liberal education: The case for it spelled out in John Henry Newman's *The Idea of a University.* But what can a series of lectures prepared by a Catholic priest for a mostly Catholic audience in Dublin in 1852, designed to persuade his audience to support the development of a Catholic university in Ireland, say to the theme of our discussions? In those lectures Newman proposed what has remained the most commonly repeated definition of liberal education: the pursuit of that knowledge which can be sought for its own sake and no further purpose. And he argued that it is this education that is the proper and exclusive concern of the university properly understood. But this argument and the refutation of the opposing view that would make "the useful arts and sciences its direct and principal concern" take up only four of the nine discourses making up Newman's original lecture series. Newman began his discourses by addressing another question: Whether "it is consistent with the idea of University teaching to exclude Theology from a place among the sciences which it embraces." And, what is less often noted or deliberately ignored by those who cite Newman's discourses, we find here a powerful argument for the inclusion of theology in the curriculum, both because its omission contradicts the very idea of the university as the home of universal learning and because in its absence other properly partial disciplines inevitably claim themselves to be universal. And finally having answered these two questions to his own satisfaction, Newman takes up another issue that is critical for our theme. In the ninth of his lectures Newman acknowledges that the natural product of a liberal education even, or especially, where that education is understood as Newman understands it, and even in the university whose curriculum has included theology, is not the Christian much less the Catholic Christian; it is rather the gentleman, or the philosopher. The university Newman proposes does not avoid all argument between the friends and foes of religion as Tocqueville's American democrats do: it rather welcomes or even lives the conflict between the life lived in accordance with Biblical revelation and what Newman calls philosophic morality.[8] Invoking this *Idea* of the university, I want to recall another observation of Leo Strauss. The life of western civilization, Strauss once said, is constituted by the tension between revelation and philosophy. No synthesis of those two is possible, he said, and so it is required of each of us to live this conflict as a philosopher open to the challenge of theology, or a theologian open to the challenge of philosophy.[9] It seems to me reasonable to describe Newman in Strauss's terms as a theologian open to the challenge of philosophy, and the university he outlined in his discourses as one that would live that tension. Can the university in America live that tension?

NOTES

1. I have used Allan Bloom's translation (New York: Basic Books, 1991) for the most part but modified it on occasion when my point requires it.

2. The words quoted appear in the essay "What is Liberal Education?" and become the explicit theme of a second essay, "Liberal Education and Responsibility." Both are included in Strauss's *Liberalism Ancient and Modern* (New York: Basic Books, 1968).

3. References are to *De la Démocratie en Amerique* . . . ed. Françoise Mélonio (Paris: Bouquins Éditions Robert Laffont, 1986), and in square brackets to the translation of Harvey Mansfield and Delba Winthrop (Chicago: University of Chicago, 2000).

4. Allan Bloom, *The Closing of the American Mind* (New York: Simon and Schuster, 1987), 246.

5. The acceptance of the "idea of the superior" in aristocracy and its denial in democracy as these are understood by Tocqueville could, I think, be restated

employing a story Machiavelli tells in his *Discorsi* (1. 47). The many in Capua, it seems, had been long oppressed by the senatorial class of that city. Finally, one Pacuvius Calanus took things into his own hands in order to reconcile the people and the senators. He locked up the senate in the palace, called the people together, and told them they might now avenge themselves on their oppressors. He persuaded them, however, that they would need new senators to replace the old ones. He suggested they proceed to an election from among themselves and execute each of the incumbents in turn as his replacement was agreed to. Looking closely at one another the people found themselves unable to agree to any new senators. At length, they agreed to the restoration of the old senators who were much chastened by the whole experience. One could say that the people denied the idea of the superior among themselves for they knew they were *semblable,* but were willing to admit the possibility of superiority even among their oppressors. In democracy proximity has eliminated that possibility.

6. "Quelque effort d'esprit que l'on fasse pour éprouver l'utilité de la vertu, il sera toujours malaisé de faire bien vivre un homme qui ne veut pas mourir."

7. "Chez l'homme, l'ange enseigne à la brute l''art de se satisfaire" (529, [521]).

8. This issue is explored more fully in John Goyette and William Mathie, "The Idea of a Catholic University: Newman on the Role of Theology in a Liberal Education," *Maritain Studies* 16 (2000), 71–91.

9. Thomas Pangle, ed., *The Rebirth of Classical Political Rationalism* (Chicago: University of Chicago Press, 1989), 270.

7

Human Dignity and Higher Education Today

Peter Augustine Lawler

The fundamental fact of our time is the gradual encroachment of principled individualism—or unregulated personal freedom—into all areas of our lives. That means that every moral and communal certainty—except those that can be justified through contract and consent—has been transformed into a question. The great human institutions that shape the character of human beings—the family, the church, the local community, and the country—are weaker than ever. So, more than ever, human selves aren't shaped into souls through the formation or habituation Aristotle says is the source of moral virtue. Young people, more than ever, don't come to colleges with characters formed by firsthand experience. They show up at college more seeking— rather than bringing—selves or souls. They don't know who they are, and so they don't know what to do. They don't know what it means to live a personally significant or dignified life.

The experience of the young is, increasingly, that every human attachment is basically voluntary. Life is all about designing oneself according to an ever-expanding menu of choice provided by an increasingly free, prosperous, and globalizing society. A choice, they think, is nothing more or less than a preference, and nobody can tell an individual why he or she should prefer this rather than that, as long as he or she doesn't violate the rights of another free chooser. Deep down, our students don't know whether they are or will be parents, children, creatures, citizens, or friends. All they're told is that in our wonderful, enlightened, high-tech world, such commitments are up to them. They're coming to college with the sense that their options have been kept open, and with a real but weak sense that eventually some of them will have to close.

Professors, meanwhile, used to think they were all about the shaping of souls. They used to believe their main job was to pass on the truth embedded in a religious tradition or the truths embedded in a traditional moral code—one that was often some version of classical or Stoic thought—that should thoughtfully define the lives of educated gentlemen and ladies. Or at least they thought, Anthony Kronman explains in *Education's End*, that their job was to open students' eyes to the alternative forms of human excellence displayed in the greatest works of philosophy and literature: the saint, the philosopher, the poet, the warrior, the inventor, the entrepreneur, the scientist, and the statesman. It was obvious that these models of human excellence were more than whimsical preferences. Jesus, Socrates, Washington, Shakespeare, Newton, Lewis and Clark, and Marcus Aurelius all differed in important ways about the definition of human excellence and who an excellent person must be. But appreciating the nobility or dignity of each of these men is one mark of any educated person. Professors used to think it was obvious that every human life is a dramatic display of a free and responsible human soul choosing between good and evil on the tough and risky journey to moral perfection. The morally challenging fact is that the line between good and evil runs through every human soul which is the foundation of our dignity.

Professors used to think students needed both their guidance and that of the models of human greatness they could reveal to them to discover who they are and what to do. One irony, of course, is that when professors offered such guidance, students didn't particularly need or want it. They came to college with their character already formed, already habituated to the practice of moral virtue. In those days, the real experience of professors was often a kind of blithe irresponsibility that came with moral impotence. They could say what they wanted without the fear of doing all that much harm—or all that much good. In many cases, students thought, with good reason, that their professors, at least, were basically reinforcing what they already knew from firsthand—or not merely bookish—communal experience.

Today's students, we can say, are often stuck with being searchers. They are—or might be—particularly open to the traditional claim of liberal education which asserts: We can find the answers to the questions concerning human identity and through reading and talking about those books that take those questions with an amount of genuine seriousness. By default, we might say, college is stuck with the job that religion—the Bible and churches—used to do. Today's college at their secular best—at, say, Great Books places like St. John's—education is about articulating the perennial human questions for young men and women who clearly don't know the truth about the dignified direction their lives should take. But even Great Books education has mor-phed into the celebration of the questions in the absence of real answers. Who can be satisfied with merely celebrating the questions or reveling in the impotent indecision of Socrates about who we are and what to do? Great Books education—detached altogether from any religious or (very broadly speaking) Stoic context—seems to present us with the alternatives of being a self-knowing philosopher and losing oneself in either fundamentalist dog-matism or aimless relativism. But the searcher doesn't really need or want to be told that the point of life is searching. Or that, as Allan Bloom claims in *The Closing of the American Mind*, the only real point of life is being a Socratic philosopher, which means, in part, getting over illusions about per-sonal significance.

So another irony is that at a time when students, more than ever, long for more guidance than could possibly be provided by their teachers, professors no longer believe that they have what it takes to provide it. Sometimes, they still think that they're charged with liberating the students from "the cave" or traditional or religious or bourgeois conformity to think for themselves. Yet, they must at least half-way know that their empty dogmas of non-conformism or self-creation or promiscuous libertarianism are a large part of the cave of any free and prosperous society.

The Americans, as Tocqueville wrote, are Cartesians without ever hav-ing read a word of Descartes; methodical doubt is the natural approach of a democrat who believes that "nobody is better than me." But there are no more conformist slaves of fashion than members of a society formed by the doctrine that nonconformity—or merely questioning authority—is the bottom line. The good news, the American democrat naturally thinks, is that nobody is better than me, but the bad is that I'm no better than anyone else, and so he or she no real point of view by which to resist the pressure of the anonymous public opinion. "Think for yourself" and "Be Creative" are, by themselves, hardly the best advice for establishing personal dignity in times like ours, in times when everyone is skeptical of claims for personal virtue.

Our professors often seem to live fairly traditional lives themselves. They have certainly become more bourgeois or careerist and a lot less bohemian or countercultural. What even the so-called tenured radicals say about liberation and non-judgmentalism is often contradicted by their ordinary, tenured lives. But like most Americans, they don't believe they have any right to impose—meaning defend with any authority—their preferences about personal moral-ity on others. They proclaim a principled indifference to the character of students' souls. They don't think it's the job of specialized scholars to take the place of parents. What scholars know is too narrow, provisional, and impersonal to guide the whole lives of young people.

LIMITLESS FREEDOM—A HOSTILE ENVIRONMENT

So where our professors used to be stuck with moral impotence, they now embrace it as a theory that justifies their irresponsibility. Students, more than ever, are free to choose in all areas of their lives in college. They have almost limitless freedom in choosing what to study, and hardly anything moral or intellectual is required of them. What few requirements that are imposed on students are as broad and flexible as to point them in no particular direction at all. In the name of freedom and diversity, little goes on in college that gives them any guidance concerning who they are or what to choose.

Students, in fact, are often taught that what they do is both completely voluntary and utterly meaningless. They're even taught that their freedom to choose is close to unlimited and completely unreal. The human person has no real existence in the wholly impersonal nature described by our scientists. Students learn from neuroscientists that "the soul" must always be put in quotes, because it doesn't correspond to any material or chemical reality. From biologists, they learn that what particular individuals or members of species do is insignificant or makes no real difference to the flourishing of our species. The flourishing of species is the point of all natural reality.

Sometimes our students learn that although the self or the "I" is really an illusion, it's one we can't live without. According to the evolutionary scientist Daniel Dennett, belief in human dignity is indispensable for the flourishing of members of our species. So, we should embrace that belief in view of its beneficial social consequences. But it's still the case that there's nothing real backing up any confidence we might have in personal importance, just as there's nothing real backing up our experiences of love or free will. We need to call true, our philosopher Richard Rorty explained, those illusions that make us feel free, comfortable, and secure. And one way to do that, Rorty adds, is not to believe the scientists when they compare our personal experiences to some objective truth. By saying that "truth" must always appear in quotes, we avoid disparaging what we choose to believe by comparing it with real standard.

Despite the best efforts of talented professors, students, it goes without saying, never really realize that the "I"—the reality of the person each of sees in the mirror—doesn't exist. They can't really reduce what they think they know about themselves as particular beings with names and personal destinies to merely useful illusions. So, the main effect of higher education is to show each of them how really alone in a hostile environment he or she is. There's no better way to convince someone of his or her utter isolation than to tell him that you—meaning your personal experiences—don't really exist, although it's okay if you pretend that you do. That's why, from the point of view of profound outside observers, such as the great anticommunist dissident Aleksandr Solzhenitsyn—it's easy to hear the howl of existentialism just beneath the surface of our happy-talk pragmatism. In part, our students are so lonely because they don't think they have the words—only howls of desperation—to describe truthfully who they are to others.

And despite all the therapeutic efforts to build inclusive and diverse communities, our colleges are often very lonely places. Because our highest educators believe they have no authority to rule the young, they've allowed our campuses, in many respects, to revert to a kind of state of nature, something like the war of all against all for the scarce resource of personal significance or dignity. There, as Tom Wolfe has described in *I am Charlotte Simmons*, the strong and beautiful "hook up," the weak and ugly are condemned to "sexile," the clever use their cunning to master the fraudulent arts of networking and teambuilding or to become trendy, marketable intellectuals, and the timid and decent are shown the vanity of their slavish moral illusions. Meanwhile, administrators look on with politically correct non-judgmental cluelessness about how their officially egalitarian and inclusive doctrine has liberated their charges for ruthless competition with necessarily inegalitarian results.

Students are stuck with using all means available to establish who they are through their successes in manipulating and dominating others. Of course, they're also stuck with being able to distinguish between how they "dress for success" and who they really are, between the self they construct to impress themselves upon others and the self that stands behind the constructed selves. So, no matter how much a student succeeds in establishing his or her importance in the eyes of others, he or she is stuck, in some ways, with being more lonely and undignified than ever. They are characterized, perhaps more than ever, by the inauthentic emptiness Christopher Lasch described in *The Culture of Narcissism*.

All in all, it seems that today's student gets to college more free in the sense of lost or empty or more disoriented than ever, and the effect of college, in most cases, is to make him or her more lost. It's still not true that the graduate ends up believing that freedom really is having nothing left to lose, because the personal self or soul and its longings are more exposed than ever. They may be told that they're stuck with self-creation, but they are not God. They can't create themselves out of nothing, and so they can't help but know that they're more than nothing, although without any clear of view of who are what that might be.

So our colleges don't really deny the reality of personal freedom. They assume to be true or leave intact the two dominant understandings of freedom and dignity in our technological society—productivity and autonomy. Productivity is the standard of the techno-majors chosen by an overwhelming

majority of our students—from engineering to the health sciences to marketing and public relations. Autonomy dominates the soft social sciences—such
as sociology and women's studies—and the humanities.

According to the philosopher Hobbes, our dignified freedom is displayed
in our productivity, in our generation of power in opposition to nature, in
what we can do that commands a price. Nature, in truth, treats each of us with
a most cruel indifference. She accords persons no dignity at all. But, we can
use our freedom to change our natural environment to make our particular
existences more secure, and that's the only change we should believe in. For
Hobbes, the point of freedom is to generate power to not not be. Nature is
out to kill me in all sorts of ways, and so to secure my dignity I have to get
to work and do something about that.

According to the philosopher Kant, Hobbes assumes that each human individual regards himself as unique and irreplaceable. So his dignity couldn't
possibly be found in his productivity or price, in being just another natural
resource. Our dignity is found in our ability to act freely against natural
instinct and inclination, and we do so by respecting the dignity of other free
beings which are able to do the same. Our dignity is in our autonomy, in our
moral freedom, in our ability to tell ourselves, in freedom, what to do.

Hobbes and Kant really aren't that opposed to each other. They both agree
that our dignity can only be found in our freedom from nature, and that
there's nothing dignified in living according to nature. They both say that
the human being is on his or her own to acquire his freedom or dignity, and
that God and nature—and even community and tradition—can provide no
authoritative guidance for who we are.

For Hobbes, our common political life is an invention by free beings to
achieve a level of personal security which has not been given to us by nature.
After we've achieved a certain level of security and prosperity, each of us is
on his or her own to live as he or she pleases with no natural guidance. We
are free, as Maslow says, to pursue self-actualization, to discover or invent
the "real me" who is more than a mere body. Kant does say that the only way
to be free from nature or selfish interest and inclination is to act rationally and
morally. But today's proponent of autonomy is satisfied to say that anything
a free being chooses is dignified. And so the productivity unleashed by technological progress serves autonomy by expanding the number of free choices
possible in our lives.

Most sophisticated graduates of our better colleges today—those David
Brooks called bourgeois bohemians—take pride in both their productivity and autonomy. They both work hard and display their uniquely human
self-fulfillment through their free personal choices. They believe there's no
dignity in choosing for natural instinct, for being the species-perpetuating

machine described by Mr. Darwin. There's no dignity in being merely begetting or belonging beings, in being social, gregarious animals. Being autonomous means refusing to be defined by what comes naturally, by, for example, having babies. That's why today's productive and autonomic woman is so insistent about her reproductive freedom, about resisting the tyranny of her body's baby-making equipment and her natural inclination to be a mother. That's also why our sophisticated intellectuals are so insistent about affirming the right to same-sex marriage: No free human institution can be constrained by natural or biological imperatives. Two or more autonomous beings can come together for any purpose they choose, and marriage should be nothing but the public affirmation of the dignity of that personal choice.

There's no dignity in living well with any of our natural limitations, in, for example, living well with death or being grateful for the human goods that depend upon our mortality or finite existence in this world. Productivity is about fending death off as long as possible. Nature's victory over each of us may be inevitable, but its timing is indefinite enough that there's no need for me to relax and accept the inevitability of my not being. After all, the idea of autonomy points in the direction of implacable hatred of our bodies and the control they have over us. So, our autonomy freaks are in rebellion against all those institutions that our bodily limitations seem to make necessary and good—such as the family, the nation, and the church. The autonomous being aims to live in cosmopolitan detachment from all those particular constraints and to live a free or sort of ghostly existence nowhere in particular.

Productivity and autonomy both point in the direction of "transhumanism" or toward a free existence unlimited by bodily constraints. That means that both productivity and autonomy are both un- and anti-erotic. The experience of incompleteness that animates the various forms of love is undignified. The modern techno-view of freedom is to be disembodied, and disembodied eros is surely an oxymoron. Even God had to become man to display his personal love for each of us. In addition, even Socrates said philosophy is learning how to die, which is just about impossible to do if you don't have a body.

The imperatives of productivity and autonomy both suggest that there's dignity in separating sex from birth or death and so making it an absolutely free expression of who I am. The productive view—the one put forward by our college administrators—is that the only limitations to sexual behavior should be *safety* and *consent*. A free being does what he or she pleases so long as he or she doesn't bring a free being into existence, cause a free being's demise, or tyrannize over another free being. Of course, a productive being also doesn't allow love to get in the way of work. An autonomous being refuses to allow love—the result of mere biological instinct run amok—to produce undignified or unfree behavior. So it's no wonder that we seem to

live in a particularly *unerotic* time: Neither the productive nor the autonomous being can extend his or her autonomous imagination to include families, children, countries, or maybe even real friends and lovers.

Maybe that's why food has become more exciting—more a dangerous
liaison and risky business—than sex. We're increasingly paranoid, puritanical, and prohibitionists when it comes to food from a health and safety
perspective. Gluttony is a vice that can kill you, or at least make you fat
and so less pretty, pleasing, and productive. Sex can kill you only if you get
mixed up with too much love—like in the case of Romeo and Juliet—or if
it is unprotected. The Bourgeois bohemian says the truth is that you get too
much safe, recreational sex, and it's puritanical and prohibitionist to think
otherwise. How bohemian could it be to make sex that unerotic and food that
scary? "Safe sex" is the bourgeois view of sex, and obsessive calorie and carb
counting is the bourgeois view of food.

To see how fundamentally un-bohemian our alleged bourgeois bohemians
are, you have to look no further than the trendy TV show *Mad Men* (about
Manhattan advertising executives around 1960): These *Mad Men* smoked,
they drank lots of martinis day and night, they only exercised when they
thought it was fun, and they had all sorts of reckless extramarital liaisons.
We can see they were *mad* because they lacked caution in their pursuit of
personal self-fulfillment. Today's sophisticates are so un-bohemian that the
advertising executives of the recent past look like bohemians in comparison
with us. In the lives of our students and teachers, the conflict between being
bourgeois and being bohemian has withered away only because productivity
trumps autonomy at every turn.

THE ORIGIN OF THE BOURGEOIS BOHEMIAN

The conflict between being bourgeois and being bohemian was previously
displayed as evidence of the limits of the American idea of freedom. For a
while, college professors and students seemed to be divided between those
who aimed to be productive and those who aimed to be artistically self-
fulfilled. We learn from books and movies such as *Revolutionary Road* that
our 1950s suburbs were full of people who were boring and desperately conformist, people incapable of living interesting lives. We used to think that the
people who earned the money didn't know how to live, and those who chose
la vie boheme couldn't even pay the rent. And, the bohemians criticized our
multiversities for producing corporate techno-cloned other-directed organization men, while often dropping out of college themselves to soar higher than
their professors. Even Bohemian Tories with a genuine concern for living

well, such as the conservative Russell Kirk, sometimes dropped out of an increasingly bureaucratized and standardized university system.

The bohemian critics of the 1950s were already making the criticisms of technocratic education for productivity we make today. The American university was lacking a unifying vision of a whole human life, and it was incapable of preparing young people for the art of life. They noticed that only scientific and technical courses were taken seriously as conveying real knowledge. They were the classes all about "facts," where the humanities were all about emoting mere "values." Autonomy or self-actualization was presented as nothing more than whimsical self-indulgence, as nothing real.

The theorists of the 1960s claimed that education for productivity had become obsolete. The techno-conquest of scarcity now allows the surrender of bourgeois discipline for unprecedented liberation of huge numbers of people to "Do their own thing." The "how" or the acquisition of the material means for living a good life had become easy. So, we had become free not to be guided by the necessity of obsessing over productivity in choosing how to live. The Sixties' theorists agreed with the proponents of productivity that there was no returning to the repression and prejudice of the past. Capitalism, they assumed whether they knew or it not, had discredited all past standards and ways of life. So they thought of themselves as both freed by and from productivity for imagining a wholly unfrequented vision of free or unconstrained self-fulfillment.

The view of the bourgeois 1950s establishment suggested that all virtue that doesn't contribute to productivity is repressive or "surplus," and the indispensable families and religion were reconfigured in a sort of utilitarian direction by the social scientific brigade of our organization men. The bohemian claim of the Sixties' theorists was that even virtue that served productivity is "surplus," and so reason, freedom, creativity, and love could be liberated, for the first, from alienating distortions. The true meaning of bourgeois success is that many people are now free to be bohemian without experiencing the downsides of judgmental marginalization and material deprivation.

The Sixties' theorists miss the irony of what's most true in Marx: Capitalism makes human beings miserably anxious by turning every human purpose, except those that serve productivity, into a meaningless whim. The Sixties' theorists, we can say, made us more miserably anxious or disoriented still by reducing even bourgeois virtue to meaninglessness. Despite their best efforts at being creative, their thinking really did culminate in the anarchist or nihilist conclusion that freedom really is just a word for nothing left to lose. They certainly gave us no new support for our longings for personal significance or dignity. Their view of freedom was really the same as that found in Marx's description of the communism to come: Life is nothing but a series of disconnected, unobsessive pursuits that have no meaning beyond immediate enjoyment.

The 1960s intellectual rebellion rightly began against the technocratic view that factual statements always begin not with "I think," but rather with "studies show." Real knowledge is always to be expressed impersonally, and so has nothing to do with who real people are and what they are supposed to do. But by the end of the 1960s, "studies show" courses in the social sciences and humanities were replaced by aggressively personal and merely subjective "studies" courses—black studies, women studies, and so forth. These courses were based on the premise that human identity is nothing more or less than an assertion of power, and that, as Hobbes says, that there's no truth, only power. So "studies" courses, unwittingly, reinforced Hobbes' bourgeois lesson: My dignity depends upon my power and nothing more. And taking "studies" courses is no way to prepare oneself to live a genuinely powerful or productive and so dignified life. Anyone who really believes what's taught in a "studies" course would switch over to a technical major, and surely that's what many blacks and women did who genuinely craved dignified liberation.

The scientists and technocrats are usually aware enough that the clarity of their studies comes from abstraction from all perceptions of personal reality. And they were certainly right in concluding that "studies" courses are nothing more than emotional outbursts of "value" that correspond to nothing real. So the progress of science and technology was never really challenged by the know-nothing propaganda coming from the social sciences and humanities in the late 1960s. The effectual truth of the 1960s was to empty the humanities of much of their real content—which came from taking virtue seriously as more than a way to productivity or autonomy. That meant humanities courses became, on balance, less challenging and even less interesting to students as real alternatives to the domination of productivity (or "quantitative assessment") in higher education. Autonomy, to say the least, failed to liberate itself from productivity.

Nor did autonomy in the form of Sixties' liberationist really discredit the virtues connected with productivity. One contradiction of Sixties' radicalism is that its new "art of living" both depended upon and rejected the disciplined habits and social institutions that make possible techno-prosperity. Those radicals embraced, naively, a key error of Marx, who believed, for no clear reason, that the conquest of nature can occur once and for all, allowing the alienation associated with the division of labor responsible for the conquest to wither away.

The conquest of past scarcity, as the libertarian Brink Lindsey patiently explains in *The Age of Abundance,* continues to depend on people doing what's required to be productive. To be productive, people continue to have to be calculating, inventive, flexible, industrious, pleasing, and capable of abstract or impersonal loyalty, thoughtful and disciplined enough to defer gratification today for an even better tomorrow, stuck with anxious stress of competition, and genuinely willing to accept the alienation that comes with the division of labor. And the dignity that comes with practicing the bourgeois virtue is more real, of course, than any associated with merely un-obsessively doing one's own thing.

THE REAL LESSON OF THE SIXTIES

The real lesson of the Sixties is that we can't dispense with the virtues that empower us to be free from nature for doing what we please when we're not working. Our neocons and New Democrats of the seventies, eighties, and nineties taught us that deviance, dysfunction, and the pseudo-profundity of romantic bohemian sentimentalism are all self-indulgent and self-destructive vices, at least if they flourish at the expense of personal productivity.

But, from our sophisticated bourgeois bohemian view, there's still much to appreciate about Sixties' transformations in the direction of autonomy. The moral repression that had nothing to do with and, in fact, inhibited productivity was overcome. The freedom of individuals from the arbitrary categories of race, class, gender, and even sexual orientation was undeniably progress. So too was the liberation of sexual appetites from pointless guilt, shame, and ignorant frustration, as was even their desublimation in the direction of commodification. From a bourgeois bohemian view, Sixties' progress included luring women out of the home and into the workplace in the name of both autonomy and productivity, heightened skepticism about traditional religious dogmas, and a new openness—even through the use of soft and safe recreational drugs—to demystified, Aquarian, New Agey forms of spirituality. So, for our colleges today, it's clear what was good about the Sixties. That decade's new forms of autonomous self-fulfillment have been safely reconfigured to be perfectly compatible with health, safety, and productivity.

Our libertarian thinkers, like Tyler Cowen in *Creative Destruction: How Globalization is Changing the World's Cultures*, are best at explaining what the bohemian side of bourgeois bohemian means now. Our techno-globalizing world makes it possible for prosperous people to be appreciative and tasteful consumers of the products of a diverse array of cultures. It's easier than ever to enjoy the food, music, literature, and art of other cultures without having to be actually dragged into the repressive morality and limited, un-individualistic horizon of any particular culture. It's surely wonderful to be able to consume

French food without having to be saddled with all the emotional baggage that comes with actually being French, just as it's wonderful to admire the art of Papua New Guinea without having to engage in the sweaty, risky business of hunting and gathering and fighting and being haunted by the imaginary presence of evil spirits.

Today's bohemian is a multiculturalist, finding self-fulfillment from the relatively un-obsessive but still meaningful perspective of the tourist or hobbyist exploring the huge and diverse menu of good things the world has to offer. That's why the study of world religions has become so popular; it's basically unthreatening fun to learn about all the sundry gods and goddesses without being stuck with all the love, cruelty, fear, and tough personal discipline that comes with actually believing in any of them. Such enjoyment is perfectly compatible with the individualistic view that every human endeavor is to be voluntary or freely chosen, and its evidence of the individual's freedom from defining his whole life according to productivity or the necessity of alienating work. The free individual, in fact, is free from the puritanical moral obsessiveness that would make a life a "whole." His personal life is characterized by diverse self-fulfilling enjoyments that don't need to be ranked, as long as he or she remembers that his autonomy depends on his productivity. He claims not to have to know who he or she is—beyond being a productive being—to know how to live.

Cowen retains some of the Sixties' confidence that a free society will not only consume—but produce—high culture, because of all the liberated reason, freedom, creativity, and love. But mostly he seems to acknowledge the irony that the globalizing conditions that produce the unfettered consumption of culture by good producers will also undermine the real diversity of cultures in the world. The growth of diversity on the individual level tends to level diversity on the social or cultural level. Eventually, of course, the effects will even be bad for diversity on the individual level. Of course, we can't withhold individualistic enlightenment from various cultures for that reason—that would be holding some in "cultural slavery" for the enjoyment of freer individuals. We can hope, the libertarian can perversely add, that some people will remain irrational or tribal enough to keep real cultural diversity alive against the forces of enlightenment. We can appreciate as consumers—but not imitate or even condone as free beings—people who choose an understanding of dignity or significance that's something other than autonomy or productivity.

The old bohemians, of course, meant to be genuinely countercultural, to define themselves authentically as whole artistic or poetic or even religious beings against bourgeois productivity or an empty view of autonomy that's indistinguishable from productivity. They claimed to know who they are and what they are supposed to do with their lives. And they willingly and even irresponsibly sacrificed careerist productivity for personal, self-fulfilled, purposeful happiness. That meant, of course, they seemed, like Socrates, to live like parasites off of the productive. But we still looked to them for some alternative guidance for what human life is for, because we sometimes believed them when they said they had a clue about human meaning or purpose.

THE END OF THE HUMANITIES? THE END OF HUMANITY?

Today's "postmodern" humanist professors don't even claim to some "holistic" view of the art of human life, although they still enjoy the perks of professors who thought they could offer people real guidance. Stanley Fish, one our most notable practitioners and defenders of liberal education, sees in his ironic way that privileges without responsibility can't last long. Fish, in "The Last Professor," acknowledges that our universities are, more than ever, defined by the "ethic" of measurable productivity and efficiency. Increasingly, the humanities seem impractical and unaffordable. Higher education, it would seem, need not waste time and money on teaching students how to enjoy the products of other cultures tastefully. They can pursue their hobbies on their own. The faculty member, Fish also observes, who "delivers insight and inspiration" is obsolete, because neither he nor his bosses really believe he has the warrant to tell students what to do or how to live.

Fish doesn't spend enough time blaming himself for this state of affairs: He admits he doesn't believe he teaches anything real, and yet he still wants what he does to be given non-instrumental value, to be cherished in its "inutility." Despite himself, he accepts the "business model" of the university administrators: What doesn't generate power or productivity isn't real. He doesn't defend the traditional proposition that what we most need to know in order to live well can't be measured. In his view, it would seem that professors like himself can and should disappear because they do not know the true standard of human significance or dignity that trumps productivity. Because of the emptiness of the autonomous alternative to productivity they promote, professors of humanities have just about put themselves out of business.

It's easy to criticize the bourgeois bohemian product of our colleges and universities for his or her superficiality. Some critics, such as Allan Bloom, say we're producing generations of emotional solitaries—people unable to be moved to thought or action by love or death. By raising and teaching the young as if they didn't have souls, we're producing souls that are flat or one-dimensional. They're not lost or homeless, but all too at home in a world made for emotional tourists, for being at home everywhere because they're not at home anywhere in particular.

But there's actually more truth to what Solzhenitsyn says about our pragmatism barely concealing the howl of existentialism: People are, and experience themselves, as more alone than ever. We really do, more than ever, have a meritocracy based on productivity, which means the pressure is on like never before to be productive. These are the best times ever to be young, smart, pretty, flexible, and industrious, but the pressure is on to display those qualities to avoid loneliness and possess dignified significance. Not only that, people are full of moral anxiety. They know, for example, that they've been given the responsibility to raise their kids to be more than productive beings; to have more than the survival skills required to flourish in the competitive marketplace. But, unless they've turned to very personal religion, they have no idea who either they or their kids ought to be or what people should be raised to do.

DIGNITY AS PRODUCTIVITY AND
BIOTECHNOLOGICAL TYRANNY

Somebody might say that anxiety is a small and whiny price to pay for maximizing individual liberty. Freedom from nature is bound to have its unpleasant side effects, although it's still much better than submitting to the brutish undignified fate nature has in store for each of us. But it's also true that our inability to find a standard of personal dignity or significance to trump productivity might be the foundation for a new birth of tyranny in the emerging biotechnological world.

Consider that a perfectly technological world would be one in which every natural resource was harnessed to maximize the productivity of free beings. Biotechnology, in effect, adds one's own body to the list of natural resources, and the philosopher of unregulated individualism, John Locke, did say that my body is my property to be exploited at will with security and enjoyment in mind. Biotechnology promises to make the transhumanist dream of not being determined by our bodily limitations, of giving orders to our bodies the way we do to any animal we've domesticated for our benefit, into a reality.

This insight is the source of our enthusiasm today for cosmetic surgery and cosmetic neurology. It would seem that enhancing the body of a perfectly healthy individual would be a violation of the Hippocratic Oath—which says, in effect, don't turn someone into a patient for reasons that have nothing to do with health. These days, autonomy seems to trump such traditional concerns. But what are the main reasons that people nip, tuck, Botox, and all of that?

To look younger and more pleasing and so to be more productive? To avoid the insignificance and indignity of being old, alone, and poor? Autonomy is subordinated to dignity understood as productivity. And if there's nothing wrong with such physical enhancement, the pressure is going to be on us all to be young and pretty as long as we can be, which will be a lot longer than nature intends. Autonomy, in effect, will be sacrificed to productivity.

The same will be true of ways to improve our cognitive abilities, our memories, and our moods with productivity in mind. Consider the example of the notoriously autonomy-obsessed and unproductive professor. We used to tolerate a good deal of professorial moodiness—despite the fact he or she drove off students and was too disoriented to publish to his or her fullest potential—for two reasons. We didn't think professors could help it; they're screwed up by nature. And we sort of bought the claim that we all—and profound people especially—have a right to our "natural moods" as an indispensable clue to the truth about who we are. Bad moods especially—such as anxiety—might lead us in the direction of the truth about being and human being.

But what if professors could easily find a safe and reliable chemical remedy for their moodiness? Deans might start to say "we'll keep you around only if you brighten up." The professor might object, "I have a right to my moods! They lead me to the truth." But, the dean would patiently respond: "Moods are nothing but random collections of chemicals, and we free beings aren't bound by any 'natural' reason to privilege one collection of chemicals over another. So we have no reason not to choose the ones that lead us towards being productive, and there's no reason why these moods can't be called true." Autonomy is the justification for allowing moods to be enhanced, but mere autonomy is not going to be enough to trump productivity in the free choice of moods.

If we can't find a standard of dignity or personal significance that's more truthful and secures our significance better than autonomy and productivity, then biotechnology, in truth, is not really going to give us a new birth of freedom. More than ever, it's going to subject us to the lonely and one-dimensional standards of health, safety, and productivity. There will be no reason not to enhance the real bohemian and the old-fashioned professor of the humanities out of existence.

DIGNITY AND HIGHER EDUCATION

It's no secret that most of our colleges that give lip service to "liberal education" don't deliver it, and what they do teach exaggerates—not moderates—the undignified confusion of our time. They certainly don't give students the impression that there's much—if any—moral or humanistic "content" (versus "method"—such as critical thinking or analytical reasoning) that they need to know. And so they don't give students the impression that their education is about whom they are or what they're supposed to do. Not only that, the permissive and indulgent atmosphere of our colleges extends adolescence far more than it serves as a bridge between being a playful child and assuming the responsibilities of an adult. Everyone knows that our colleges teach habits that are positively antagonistic to the formation of moral virtue and often undermine the good habits and confident beliefs students sometimes actually bring with them to college.

So Charles Murray, in *Real Education*, seems on strong ground when he argues that we should declare the brick-and-mortar college obsolete for most purposes it now claims to serve. The students who go to college in pursuit of a technical career—the overwhelming majority of them—might be better served by a more focused and condensed education that would take much less than four years and wouldn't require "the residential experience." Maybe we should abandon the pretense that the B.A. is the admission ticket to the world of most white-collar work. Students might actually be less disoriented and confused if they were free from the fantasy that anything by college can give them a standard of freedom and dignity higher than productivity, and they might be better off and closer to the truth with what they've picked up from their family, their church, and their community. Liberal education—in a society that has abdicated on most fronts the project of sound "cultural transmission"— couldn't possibly function as the cure for what most ails us. Murray is surely right that the project of civic and cultural literacy belongs in grade and high school, and it's the fault of our colleges—particularly, but not only our schools of education—that it's not there. We can't expect the institutions that have eviscerated our high schools to make up for what they haven't done.

Murray concludes that "liberal education"—including real precision in the use of language and real knowledge of what's required for moral choices— might be preserved for those most likely to assume positions of political, intellectual, and economic leadership in our country. Tocqueville, we remember, said something not so different: Those with literary careers—or those charged with perpetuating key distinctions in our language—should study the Greek and Roman authors in their original language. That way our language will retain some contact with metaphysical, theological, and moral distinctions that correspond to the multi-layered truth about the human soul. Otherwise, the trend will continue to be for our language to become exclusively impersonal, vague in crucial respects, and too technical for us to say anything true about our freedom and dignity. For Tocqueville and Murray, we need a few excellent universities far more than many mediocre colleges.

This sort of conclusion is unsatisfying if we believe that every human being has a soul worthy of being educated. Everyone, of course, has to live well with the responsibilities given to begetting and belonging beings open to the truth, including the personal truths of love and death. In a time when even claims about truth and morality invites skepticism, religious training and moral habituation, by themselves, won't be enough to inspire the self-confidence and good judgment required to lives of genuine personal significance. The traditional claim of liberal education which asserts that everyone needs more than a technical education remains true. And surely it must be regarded as true if we are really to subordinate technical progress to human purposes.

Liberal education does exist here and there within our country, and it exists particularly in the smaller liberal arts colleges. In fact, most of those colleges are inspired to aim high through their vibrant religious missions, through their concern with the personal destiny of particular souls. We are most likely to find liberal education geared towards a wide variety of students in our religious colleges. No doubt, some of it is little more than apologetics to support pious indoctrination, but St. Thomas Aquinas in California, for example, is thought by many to be the best "Great Books" college in the country. Students who choose religious colleges are usually clearer about who they are than many of our lost souls when they get to college, but that doesn't mean that they don't need—really need—the kind of intellectual challenge and depth that can only come through higher education. It seems unlikely that in our time—a time without a secular moral code (or without any confidence in the reality of ladies and gentlemen) or any real moral consensus, secular colleges and universities can be up to the task of dignified liberal education in any big way. If not, the future of human dignity—or at least dignified higher education—may depend more than ever on our religious institutions.

8

Now That the University Has Become the High School, Where Do We Get an Education?

W. B. Allen

I must begin by qualifying my title. The important issue is what we think education is to begin with. I answered that question in two brief passages in my *Habits of Mind*[1], a context for which should make the passages more accessible. A familiar hotel sign helps to set that context. It enables us to recover the forgotten and now implicit reference to aristocracy in every discussion of higher education. Nevertheless, we are democrats—more than democrats, we are progressives—and we have certain expectations of ourselves and of humanity at large that we cannot compromise.

The familiar hotel sign brings this home in the form of the notice that says, "don't use the towel just once; use it two or three or four times. Save the earth." This is doubtless good counsel that we ought to follow; but why has its reach been truncated? After all it has only been a handful of years in which people have practiced daily baths. For a long time they bathed scarcely more than once a week, if that. How much more might not the earth be "saved" if folk only bathed once a week? Simply reverting to such older practices would make a genuine impact on "global warming" and many other concerning dreads.

The problem of course is that people bathe regularly now partly in response to sanitation campaigns, but probably far more profoundly in response to the fact that it is no longer the privilege of aristocrats to bathe regularly. Once upon a time ordinary people just did not do that; only aristocrats did (and then only a few of them). This produces the following dilemma: Those who aim to save the earth nevertheless do not want to take from ordinary souls a privilege finally wrested from aristocrats. Try the thought experiment: Say to everyone, aristocrats and all, bathe once a week! Would it not be necessary to enforce it tyrannically? Instead, folk accept the reality that all are going to pursue the *appearance* of aristocracy whether they deserve it or not.

In that context a discussion of higher education deals with a transformation in culture at a deep level and from which there is no escape. It is transformation through democratization. All are democrats. Perhaps that comes from a political philosopher with ill grace; for it was at least for a long time held that political philosophy was the queen of the disciplines. One might think, therefore, that a political philosopher would be a natural aristocrat inclined to defend superior claims. However, may not a political philosopher also be aware of the necessity to discover the truth? And may not the truth be that the claims were false? It is appropriate, therefore, to deal with reality as it reveals itself when we undertake university level education.

Accordingly, we define higher education in the context in which almost everyone goes to college—almost; certainly it is true in North America, and appropriate statistics demonstrate that more and more people go to college throughout the world today. Moreover societies demand increasing participation in college (notwithstanding the current and ephemeral context of economic recession). Folk demand increasing college study for some reasons which are good, for the restructured experience of living and working has made it a necessary point of entry into useful and productive careers. Therefore societies have imposed additional requirements upon what was once regarded to be a university education, beyond the identification or recognition of what probably will always remain the handful of souls that can honestly aspire to peaks of human intellectual performance.

Let us summarize the problem: does education point to the handful of souls that can aspire to the peak of intellectual performance; or does it produce a base upon which society at large can stand and which therefore must be open to all comers; and wherein it is appropriate to encourage all to enter? Queen's University in Ontario bears the motto: *Sapientia et Doctrina Stabilitas*. Is it in fact the case that wisdom or knowledge and teaching are soundly established, stably fixed, established forever as the goal? Or does that change with changing cultural experiences and expectations?

A couple of passages in *Habits of Mind* address this question. The first is a passage that has the subheading—"why have we not realized liberal education?" It reads:

> Put most simply we fail today to realize the value of liberal education because we have lost sight of the idea of the university. The staggering growth of American colleges and universities through processes of accretion and differentiation during the past century brought with it so many new markets and missions that our universities have by and large forgotten their true purpose, their

original destination. It is outside the scope of this book to analyze every development. However six trends stand out: number one, the notion that the primary purpose of a college education is to prepare students for careers; number two, over reliance on technology as the main tool for improving student learning and for enhancing the competitiveness of the institution; number three, a lowering of academic standards mistakenly adopted as the means for expanding access to college; number four, a preference for measuring quality based on inertial growth rather than dynamic growth; number five, an incoherent curriculum particularly within the general education program; number 6, a perverse emphasis on multiculturalism and diversity in all aspects of the college experience. Each of these trends has damaged the core of the university. So analysis of their impact precedes a discussion of how to restore an idea of the university.

Now that series of observations opened the door to a discussion of whether we go to the university in order to prepare for the work world or whether we go to university in order to learn, and whether those are compatible objectives. Do men work to live or do men live to work? It is a rhetorical question. The answer of course is that men work to live; men do not live to work; and therefore it is always misguided to make work the end rather than the means to an appropriately defined human end—the end of human life. But folk in the United States at least either have lost sight of that distinction or are rarely articulate in trying to recapture it.

One of the reasons for that inarticulateness has to do with what may rightly be identified as reasons for caring about education in the first place. The section of the book titled "the legacy" directly addressed the question of access in order to get at this issue:

At a recent national gathering of faculty concerned about liberal education, one speaker offered this as an alternative title for his remarks, "less access: an idea whose time has not come."

The content of his remarks made it clear that he thought that reduced access to higher education was an idea whose time was long overdue. He suggested one specific and one general way to improve the academic performance of today's college students. His specific recommendation is not unreasonable; he urged that financial aid should be dependent upon academic performance. His general recommendation however runs contrary to the last century of higher education and to all prevailing indicators of what lies ahead in the next 100 years. His vision for restoring excellence to higher education is to limit access dramatically. But to whom would he deny access to a college education? Certainly not his own sort or his own son or daughter!

Every parent today rightly envisions a college education as part of his child's future. Nor is this a new phenomenon. Writing in 1925 J. B. Johnston described the widespread desire among parents to see their sons and daughters attend college regardless of the youths' academic accomplishments or potential. One reason this is so is that parents hope and pray for the economic success of their children. But we believe there is a more fundamental prayer being voiced, one that is consciously or unconsciously influenced by an inchoate awareness that a college education nurtures proficient humanity.

Now, meditate for a moment on the implication of that statement. Although parents encourage their youngsters to go to school and expect them to go to college and expect them to get from that a career, what remains unstated, perhaps not even fully realized within their souls, is a desire that their youngsters will attain the goal of proficient humanity. Education really is about the development of the human soul to a level of proficiency that allows us to fulfill the promises of human potential—that allows us to observe excellence attained as a result of specific exertions.

Now, if that is even remotely true, then it must be possible to capture again the idea of the university. Yes, people must learn to work and therefore prepare for careers; but that is a by-blow of the notion of attaining proficient humanity. The more important goal is to foster those concerns with the human things and the human place in the world that deepen cultural experience and enable men to preserve and therefore to pass on that cultural experience for succeeding generations. The section on the legacy, therefore, continues with the observation that the concern is not to create either widgets or robots to fit the machines to make the widgets. The concern is to sustain the progressive influence of human understanding.

To sustain the progressive influence of human understanding requires the acknowledgement that some are going to make the journey faster and better than others, and if that is true then it is important to discern how to sustain an enterprise in which those who can make the journey faster and better than others will still do so. The expression "now that the university has become the high school" means that the goal adopted at the beginning of the 20th century throughout North America—of graduating every child from high school— has now become the goal for our colleges.

And it is impressive, is it not, what was done in the 20th century? From a starting point at which 10 or 11 percent graduated high school, in less than a century—really almost by midpoint of the century—the U.S. advanced to graduating virtually everyone from high school. That is a genuine accomplishment, and it is important to ask not only how it was done, but why it was done. And it is further important to ask, ought the same objective apply to university education in the 21st century?

Perhaps it is almost too late to inquire about the 21st century, since by the end of the 20th century the proportion of Americans with some college education was already in the stratosphere—more than half. And this in spite of the fact that we still have problems in urban centers with children who drop out of high school, children who are not well-prepared—whose curricula are not pre-collegiate curricula. It is extraordinary that U.S. society accomplished that—unless one acknowledges that it was done in part by abandoning the mission of the university.

Substituting for the concern with proficient humanity, a concern with career preparation compromised the demands of the university. Is it possible to turn back the clock? I think not. And that is the most fundamental observation I have to make. I think those who want somehow to open an era of lessened access to university education are fundamentally mistaken. They are mistaken because, while consulting the educational goals of the university, they do not consult the democratic and progressive nature of our souls and our culture. What they ask is not so much to close the doors to the universities to those thought ill prepared, but to deny our progressive credentials. Folk are unable to do that. We must therefore endure the experience of widening access to the University.

But is it possible in that context still to hold fast to the motto of Queen's University? Is it possible still to hold fast to the idea of proficient humanity and the pursuit of excellence? How? Think of it even as a single class rather than the entire university for the moment. How can one stand before a cohort and offer instruction before people who are diversely prepared to receive it, and still do so honestly and credibly?

I believe there is a way to do that, and I believe that way recaptures the essence of university education. It is to remember that the process can be distinguished from the standards. It is possible to admit everyone—indeed even to practice open admission. It has always been, by the way, a curious question—for which I do not have the answer—why it is necessary for colleges and universities to select their entrants. Why are universities granted a privilege of passing over the crowd—the unwashed herd—and selecting out the ones that they are going to receive into their precincts? What connection does that have with the purpose of the university? It may have some value economically or in terms of reputation. To seek or secure the status of an elite institution, a sure method is carefully to pick only the very best, who no matter what is done to them are still going to be the very best when they leave. That works, assuredly. I spent a fair part of my career doing just that: teaching the very brightest kids and taking credit for their work! That is easy. The far tougher job is to see a crowd that is not identified as the very best and to elicit the very best from them, and simultaneously discovering within that crowd who are indeed the best and giving them the means of advance while yet addressing everyone. That is the real task; that is what the modern university faces. Let each deal with whoever presents and demonstrate how much they can accomplish then. That is a real test as opposed to loading the deck by selecting participants (or excluding challenges).

To elicit the best from the class as a whole and also to identify the best among them requires willingness to pursue the highest standards. There is no other way to do it. We must therefore encounter the risk of washing out many who come and who cannot make the full journey. We must further insist that even the learning of the least is advanced by being subjected to the greatest rigors.

Once that has been done, it may also be observed that it is possible to identify those who are going to enter that strange, ill-defined community, which spreads beyond particular universities, beyond particular societies, and which constitutes the stream of a long history that is otherwise known as the republic of letters. Ultimately the purpose of the university is to continue to populate the republic of letters and no compromise of or with that objective is acceptable, if the university is to remain a university. That means cultivating hopes, aspirations, and particular diligence in the very best. Thus, the university may yet focus on the highest aims, even while accepting the progressive obligation to work with all comers.

This truth bears expressing somewhat differently. To speak of "cultivating" requires remembering what that word means. Some things all understand, whether democrats or not, and one such is cultivation; one obtains better growth from prepared soil. It is true, however, that, when planting in sterile soils and raising stunted plants, some attention is still required. One may not produce the finest crop if one does not begin with the finest soil, but it is still a crop. It still has to be watered and fertilized in order to produce its yield. And that yield can still have some economic value.

But the finest crops will be produced—cultivated—in the finest soils. The same thing is true in higher education. We must certainly pay attention to the fullest cultivation in the best soil, but will also have to understand that we sometimes do not deal with the best soil and yet must cultivate. We do not abandon cultivation because we happen to be settled on a bad plot of land. The reason for that, of course, has to do with the association of cultivation with the word "culture." We are always engaged in the culture business. That is the most important business we engage in. Scientists and humanists alike participate in handing on a cultural inheritance that is ultimately far more valuable than any other inheritance offered to the young.

Think about this in the following way: Today people live so long that what they are likely to hand on to offspring is decreasingly relevant to the lives of those offspring, materially speaking. The latter are well middle-aged; they are successful professionals; and they have their own estates. That is how the world has changed.

The cultural inheritance works differently. Simply living longer does not produce the same advantage (or disadvantage, if one sees it so); some cultural inheritance unavoidably passes to succeeding generations. More importantly, it does so in a very peculiar way—not as net assets, but rather as an investment in future assets unknown to the donors. The heirs' discoveries, their contribution to the culture, cannot be foretold. The inheritance they receive enables them to make those discoveries, but only when handed on and only when, in particular, it sustains a secure commitment to the highest standards, to the pursuit of excellence, to proficient humanity. That is a much more important inheritance than any material inheritance. That is what keeps the dark ages away. The university is about fending off dark ages. While the university may well have become the new high school, it still performs that work. And it will do so only if it takes seriously the need to identify those who are going to continue to fend off dark ages, who are going to explore beyond frontiers, who will attain the heights of human excellence and advance proficient humanity.

Hence, I would say that the fact that the university has become high school is not dispositive. It does not settle the question. It does not change our obligations. It only changes the nature of the soil in which we labor, and I suggest serious attention to the possibility that the labor can remain fruitful even though we do not settle on the same cultivated land we once did.

The foregoing general exhortation conveys the substance of the argument in this chapter. But to be more practical, specific contemporary concerns and issues deserve clarification. In this part, therefore, I enumerate some practical themes.

An important inquiry on the topic we are considering is that which suggests the possibility that the "culture of sensitivity to the self-esteem of the young," coupled with an egalitarian impulse to award prizes to all[2] constitutes a special loss, depriving us of the instrumentalities of improvement.

This question directly addresses the heart of the discussion in *Habits of Mind* and its counsel for avoiding that very difficulty. It is certainly true in North America that folk have tried to insulate the young from failure—perhaps the biggest educational mistake made in recent decades. The analogy employed in the book highlights an area of life in which that mistake has been avoided and in which, therefore, people attain great heights. That happens to be athletics. Athletics push the individual to the point of failure. That is how they attain excellence. That is how they become "number one" (as they like to say). There, it still matters to aspire to be number one, and it is a great mystery why folk readily accept from athletics what they find intolerable in academics. For to insulate the young from failure is nothing other than a failure to exercise them—a failure to prepare them to excel. It may well be said, in reference to high school, that it is better for a student to fail calculus than never to take it. There is learning even in failing, and yet countless students never take calculus, because we insulate them from failure for fear that their self-esteem will suffer. This means that democratic souls have conquered common sense. The assumption seems to be that all must somehow share the same enjoyments and have the same degree of self-respect. Therefore a push toward the lowest common denominator follows, and no one needs to feel left out. A consequence of pursuing the lowest common denominator is to stifle full development, full accomplishment. That certainly cuts the heart out of the university.

It may well be imagined that the course counseled here compromises sympathetic efforts to tailor a world to fit the very young, as a means of nurturing or shepherding their development toward maturity. Nor would I deny that such compromises may be inherent in resisting the creation of a "kiddie sized" world. It is not unreasonable to request that, if the world does not "fit" the young, they should come to know that sooner rather than later. Why create the false appearance that the world fits them, when they require yet to grow into it? They must work to fit in, if they are to fit. If we rather make the choice of persuading youngsters that the world is tailored to their size, then they will without direction outgrow a world they imagine tailored to them. This has relevance for a discussion of higher education, insofar as lowering or watering down the standards of the curriculum amounts to furnishing the university with kiddie furniture.

That raises the next practical concern, namely, what standards ought to prevail in higher education. Again, it is possible to determine this inductively. It means something when one observes that nothing is easier than to get through Harvard University. Nothing is harder than to get in; but nothing is easier than to get through, because the fact is that not much learning goes on at Harvard. Grade inflation at Harvard is notorious. For some time its curriculum has been fairly conceived as not very challenging. More significantly, though, it occurs that graduation with a bachelor's degree from Harvard produces no significant advantage in comparison with other institutions, from which terminal bachelor's degrees have been gained. Harvard most benefits those who go on to professional and graduate education. Otherwise, their BAs are often at a disadvantage compared to many state universities in the United States. The problem: admitting the best students without requiring the best of them means that Harvard little augments the accomplishments its students had when they arrived.

Fairly, one may urge that the problem at Harvard derives from the problem of liberal education, in comparison with career education; for public institutions certainly tend far more to emphasize vocational/professional preparation over liberal education. Moreover, it often seems that understanding does not transfer across disciplines. The evidence of stellar but rare programs, such as that at St. John's College in Annapolis and Santa Fe, and the argument of works such as *The Closing of the American Mind*[3] might seem to suggest such a dilemma.

I have read closely *The Closing of the American Mind*, which makes a cogent critique of many of our practices in higher education. But ultimately I disagree with Bloom, because I believe that Bloom leans in the direction of limiting access as the only way to save higher education, which is impossible and morally wrong. However, it is true that one cannot separate what faculties do from what takes place in the university. Recently, I directed a university-wide faculty committee in redesigning an approach to general education. Such ventures recur periodically. Driving that conversation in a way that opens our understanding of the ways in which we must work as faculty across disciplines in order to achieve an educational objective is a very difficult process. The difficulty originates precisely because faculties typically work in echo chambers in which they only hear their own voices returning. The relevant issue is to escape the echo chambers in order to speak across the universe of higher education.

Programs at schools like St. John's show how that can be done. They break down the disciplinary lines, but they do not destroy the students' learning in doing so. They make a fundamental investment in student learning, forcing faculties to interact across disciplinary distinctions for the benefit of the students. Faculties rightly wonder in that context—and typically out loud—whether that means a sacrifice of professional status and research opportunity. My experience has been that it does not. In fact it can do exactly the reverse. One can be every bit as conscientious a scholar within his area if he remains mindful that the point of scholarship is to be open to challenges wherever they arise. Paying attention to things outside the discipline is actually a benefit within the discipline for the sake of advancing the discipline. One cannot generally foretell the challenges that will force a paradigm change.

There can be challenges no less significant that come from left field, that come orthogonally so to speak towards one's particular experience. So, we can validate liberal education both conceptually and also statistically by pointing to what happens to students who graduate from St. John's College and similar programs and the rate at which they enter into professional disciplines and careers. While such students do not rush into modernity, they nevertheless become very well-prepared: They all must study languages, they all must study mathematics, and somehow on the strength of having received that broad education they gain a capacity to focus when they choose to do so. This is systematically true and is one of the reasons, by the way, that a disproportionately large number of Ph.D.s in the United States originate from undergraduate programs in small liberal arts colleges.

The great universities do not comparatively produce that many Ph.D.s, i.e., people who step into the disciplines. There may be broad explanations why this is so. But it is at least true that, having been trained in liberal education, with liberal arts as their background, those who ultimately pursue disciplinary formation have found a reason to do so. From their breadth of experience and learning they are able to choose a discipline more knowledgeably than those who as undergraduates receive a narrow training. They are exposed therefore to an informed latitude of choice that might direct one to a discipline.

Perhaps one will conceive that two things seemingly contradictory occur at the same time in universities–namely, the decline of general standards of education, on the one hand, and the retention of intellectual vitality among the faculty, on the other hand. Reasoning counter-intuitively, "The Sokal Hoax[4]" may seem to validate this conclusion. Although it was designed to deflate vacuous intellectual pretension, the very conversation it sparked was taken as an instance of continuing intellectual vitality. Do we not still maintain rigorous standards in physics? Do not coaches complain that they can not attract athletes enough, because of heightened standards? In other words, is not the central premise of my argument incorrect, insofar as it requires the conclusion that universities no longer pay attention to excellence in bringing students into the university? Moreover, do not universities make special offers to gifted musicians, artists, and dancers, among others, in all which cases a standard of excellence must prevail?

It is important to remember the proviso that the university's right to choose who comes is most dubious. That is to say, the premise is not that universities do not seek excellence. They do, and everywhere I know, at least, universities practice a ritual file parsing within the pool of candidates, selecting the so-called best and admitting them. Think of this merely statistically for the moment. Sometimes we identify practices with names that do not apply to them, and one of the ways to highlight this is to inquire how it can be possible to increase from 15 percent of the population entering universities and colleges (first decade of the 20th Century) to 65 to 70 percent entering (by the end of the 20th Century) and still claim that all these institutions are selecting the best? What they select is the best *available* to them, not the best. Once choice is confined to the best available and not the best simply, it is questionable whether universities really pay attention to the true standard of excellence. Nor is it necessary to insist that any university in particular admits poor students; for it is necessarily the case that moving from 15 percent to

70 percent precludes admitting students at the same standard of performance that obtained when only 15 percent were admitted.

This paradox serves to reinforce the argument that universities should not be accorded the privilege of selecting students beyond publishing standards. Yet, even critics of contemporary practices end by reinforcing the university's claim of discretion in this regard. Critics object to affirmative action on the basis of the candidates chosen, and their supposed lack of qualification, rather than objecting to universities claims to choose in the first place. Given the broader social reality, such objections are both self-defeating and reinforcement for the worst tendencies in higher education.

Unless, then, one affects to argue that all human beings are in principle capable of performing at the highest level, the premise is not open to challenge. While I have insisted that virtually everyone can learn, and that the capacity to learn is widely spread throughout humankind, I acknowledge the reality of differential performance. But that does not require that only relatively few can perform well. It is not merely reflexive or ideological democracy that produces this conclusion. We have a sound basis for judging that most are capable of learning, and that the weightier variable is the instruction they receive, how we prepare them, how we cultivate them.

Now, it remains true that we do not have an ideal system of preparation or cultivation, and therefore that students are not generally as prepared as they need to be to function as well as possible, and that we nevertheless admit them to university. That constitutes the major premise or ground-norm accounting for the transformation of the university into the new high school.

Returning to the associated question, whether debates in the university distinguish faculties as perhaps still paying attention to the highest things, it helps to recall that postmodernism denies that there are *any* standards, denies that reason is authority, and therefore denies that we can identify any particular excellence. That creates a dilemma: It is not possible to claim a pursuit of excellence at the same time as denying any basis for identifying excellence or even that there is any such thing as excellence. The postmodern challenge does not arise in a vacuum. It occurs within the cultural experience of an attack upon and perhaps even the loss of the authority of reason.

The comforting delusion that this does not affect the technical sciences (because it is thought that natural scientists adhere to standards of reason) encourages the thinking that engineering, physics , biology are all systematic and disciplined and that they follow scientific method in a way calculated always to produce improvements. But it is not only in the moral realm that the attack on reason has its purchase; and when the philosopher Friedrich Nietzsche attacked science at the beginning of the 20th century, he attacked it at that central point at which what seemed to be discipline, what seemed to be reason, he asserted to be only will. Now the question of whether scientific method actually leads to truth or is only the construction of an elaborate willfulness, what Thomas Hobbes called a "construct of the mind," is an important question that cannot be resolved on the basis of any of the particular disciplines. That is the key: No discipline can solve the question of whether what the discipline does is rational. That stage of understanding requires a further question, beyond the disciplines: Is there still authority of reason with respect to denominating human potential? From that perspective one may identify those practices that are or are not consistent with reason in universities.

Moreover, as I speak about restoring high standards, and pointing toward proficient humanity, I mean that in the context of fostering the enjoyment of learning. That is not a practical goal. In a sense there is something more important that we engage in, namely, changing ourselves, when we undergo learning. Consummation implies attaining the point of reveling in the change.

One change would highlight the principles elaborated here more than any other, namely, open enrollment coupled with rigorous standards. That obtains at the Open University in the United Kingdom, and it is available to be considered as the basis of a general reform that would deflect attention from the entrants (and their capacities) to the successful graduates (and their accomplishments).

NOTES

This is an extensive revision of a talk originally delivered before the Queen's University Retirees' Association, January 24, 2006, Kingston, Ontario, Canda.

1. W. B. Allen and C. M. Allen, *Habits of Mind: Fostering Access and Excellence in Higher Education* (New Brunswick: Transaction Publishers, 2003).

2. This is the title of a book published in the UK in the last decade: Melanie Phillips, *All Must Have Prizes* (London : Little Brown, 1996).

3. Allan Bloom, *The Closing of the American Mind* (New York: Simon & Schuster, 1987).

4. As described in *The Skeptic Dictionary* (www.skepdic.com/sokal.html): "In its 1996 Spring/Summer issue (pp. 217–252), *Social Text* journal published an article by Allan Sokal, Professor of Physics at New York University, entitled 'Transgressing the Boundaries: Towards a Transformative Hermeneutics of Quantum Gravity.' The article was a hoax submitted, according to Sokal, to see if 'a leading journal of cultural studies [would] publish an article liberally salted with nonsense if (a) it sounded good and (b) it flattered the editors' ideological preconceptions?' It would. Needless to say, the editors of *Social Text* were not pleased."

III

The University and the Liberal Arts

9

St. Augustine, the University, and the So-Called Liberal Arts

Michael P. Foley

St. Augustine might seem an odd interlocutor for a conversation on the American university until we recall that Augustine is essentially the great-grandfather—or, depending on your genealogy, the great-great-uncle—of the university as we know it. Augustine's treatise *On Christian Doctrine* had an enormous impact on the understanding of education that led to the creation of the university in the Middle Ages, as did his thought in general. In this chapter I would like to concentrate on Augustine's critique of the liberal arts and what it can teach us about what an American university can and should be. Augustine was singularly well-suited to speak on this topic. In contrast to his autodidactic appropriation of philosophy, he not only learned at least some of the liberal arts in a formal educational setting,[1] but he also made his living teaching them: Grammar in his hometown of Tagaste, and rhetoric in the cosmopolitan centers of Carthage, Rome, and Milan. Augustine, in fact, was the first person to organize the liberal arts into the two-tiered schema that would eventually be known as the *trivium* and *quadrivium*,[2] and one of his earliest goals as a convert (which, alas, was never met) was to provide an exhaustive treatment of each of the seven liberal arts and their relationship to the Christian faith.[3]

I should mention from the start that my use of the term "liberal arts" will be largely the same as Augustine's, namely, as a designation of the seven disciplines of grammar, rhetoric, dialectic or logic, arithmetic, geometry, astronomy and music, and of the ways they were taught or understood in late antiquity. Historically, these disciplines were first called liberal because they were the privileged possession of a noble and free (*liber*) elite and because they were qualitatively different from the illiberal or servile arts, those practical skills associated with servants and the working class. Over time, however, the liberal arts also came to be seen as liberating arts, activities that freed up their practitioners from the doldrums of necessity and ignorance. Simply put, while the servile arts were for gaining a livelihood, the liberal arts were for getting a life, for living life well. It was for this reason more than any other that they were considered essential to what it meant to be educated. Even today lip service (albeit fading) continues to be paid to the liberal arts as constitutive of a real education. When Stanley Fish, for example, announced the impending death of the American university in January 2009, he did so on the basis of the decline of humanities departments and the triumph of prag-matic, utilitarian disciplines.[4] It would seem, then, that no discussion of the American university is complete without addressing the significance of the liberal arts.

THE LIBERAL ARTS IN THE WRITINGS OF AUGUSTINE

Augustine's teaching on the subject, however, is not easy to ascertain, especially given the fact that his opinion of them seems to have varied widely throughout his life. Shortly after his conversion, Augustine would write in his dialogue *On Order* that Christians who were not liberally educated could not, at least this side of the grave, be truly happy,[5] and that without the liberal arts they would botch their understanding of God and reality to the fullest extent possible.[6] But ten years later, in his *Confessions*, Augustine would strike a far less sanguine note about the power of the liberal arts. When they are mentioned by name for the first time, the reference is anything but adulatory: "I was led astray and led others astray, was deceived and deceived others . . . by the doctrines which they call liberal."[7] Augustine repeats the unflattering qualification of the liberal arts as "so-called" at the end of the same book when he writes, "And what did it profit me when I read and understood all the books of the arts which they call liberal, while I remained the vile slave of evil desires?"[8]

Rather than lead us to a well-honed knowledge of the divine, the liberal arts seem at best impotent, at worst pernicious. This critical note continues through the rest of Augustine's writings, with the "so-called" moniker used again, for example, in Epistles 26 and 101. And it reaches its zenith in the *Retractations*, written near the end of Augustine's life, where he expresses regret for the things he wrote while he was still "puffed up" with "worldly literature," presumably the liberal arts.[9] Specifically, Augustine laments that in *On Order* he "attributed too much" to the liberal arts, since people can become saints without knowing them and people who do know them are not necessarily saints.[10]

Does all this mean that not long after his conversion to Christianity, Augustine inexplicably became an enemy of the liberal arts formation that in some respects facilitated that conversion? Not quite. The *Retractations*, for example, are *not* meant to be a cool and dispassionate self-analysis. Augustine explicitly tells his reader that in this work he is approaching his earlier writings with a divine severity.[11] Inspired by St. Paul's remark, "If we judged ourselves, we should not be judged by the Lord" (I Cor. 11:31), Augustine resolves to avoid the wrath of divine judgment by being an even more exacting judge of himself.[12] This is, of course, a perfectly valid hermeneutic, but it is hardly one that gives the benefit of the doubt to possibly innocuous passages.

Similarly, Augustine's critique of the liberal arts in the *Confessions* is more a disparagement of himself at the time he was learning them than of the disciplines themselves. Augustine does not say that the liberal arts are enslaved to destructive passion, but that he was.[13] He does not say that the liberal arts taught erroneous things about God, but that he believed erroneous things about God which in turn nullified any of the liberal arts' potential benefits.[14] Indeed, later in the *Confessions* Augustine mentions figures such as Firminus and Victorinus who were able to use their liberal education for the greater glory of God,[15] and he describes the objects of the liberal arts not as demonic distractions but as truths implanted in the memory by God Himself.[16]

Finally, the dialogue *On Order* is not as roseate about the liberal arts as initially appears. Augustine explicitly states that what he calls the "order of living" must precede and accompany the order of a liberal arts education in order to attain the desired result.[17] This order involves a life of virtue, good friends, and a worshipful faith, hope, and love of the true God.[18] Without this ongoing context, we can infer, the liberal arts fall on untilled ground. Moreover, Augustine makes much ado in *On Order* about his mother Monica, who serves as a notable exception to the alleged necessity of the liberal arts. Indeed, the young Augustine attributes his own mind's love of the truth not to the liberal arts at all, but to the prayers of his pious mother;[19] and he credits Monica with leapfrogging over the intermediary stages of education to the very stronghold of philosophy itself.[20]

THE "CONS" OF THE LIBERAL ARTS

Where, then, does this leave us? It leaves us, I would argue, with a surprisingly consistent sensitivity to both the limitations and the value of the liberal arts, of both its "pros" and "cons." On the "con" side, there are significant moral, intellectual, and religious limitations to a liberal education. Morally, the liberal arts cannot save the soul from its own disordered desires, and sadly, they can easily become the occasion for a self-crippling spirit of pride and self-satisfaction. Centuries later Cardinal John Henry Newman would, with his customary eloquence, make precisely this point:

> Quarry the granite rock with razors, or moor the vessel with a thread of silk; then may you hope with such keen and delicate instruments as human knowledge and human reason to contend against those giants, the passion and the pride of man.[21]

Augustine would agree. The fecklessness of the liberal arts in the face of sin, their inability to liberate men and women from the worst kind of enslavement, is the central reason why he is loath to call them liberal.

Intellectually, the liberal arts alone do not lead to the crucial cognitional breakthrough that differentiates sensible and intelligible reality. This breakthrough, Augustine adamantly maintains, is crucial because it alone enables one to understand, however dimly, the two things most worth knowing: God and the soul.[22] Both are incorporeal, but since the mind in its day-to-day operations is accustomed to think of all reality as spatial, material, or temporal, it is ill-prepared to fathom either itself or its Maker.[23] A difficult conversion is therefore necessary, one that can turn the flesh-focused mind—to borrow a famous image from Plato—from the shadows of sensible phenomena to the luminosity of immaterial reality. According to Augustine, the heart of this conversion is the mind's discovery of itself, for when it truly understands its own understanding, it is understanding an intelligible reality;[24] and once it understands an intelligible reality, it is in a position to understand—albeit through a glass darkly—how God is not body but Spirit.[25] This in a crude nutshell is the argument of book seven of the *Confessions*, and it is significant that the catalyst singled out for this sea change in psyche are the books of the Platonists rather than any of the seven liberal arts. Indeed, Augustine states earlier that after studying the liberal arts he still remained mired in his carnal conviction that God was a sort of shiny body and he a particle broken off from it.[26]

Religiously, the liberal arts do not necessarily lead to a love of God. As we have already seen, Augustine mentions this shortcoming in his *Retractations* as a reason for no longer wishing to emphasize their importance. One reason the disciplines might not have this effect is that they are directly concerned with particular facets of knowledge rather than the Ground or Source of knowledge, which is reserved for those modes of inquiry that are at once higher and more architectonic, namely, philosophy and what would come to be known as theology. Again Newman is illuminating: "Liberal education makes not the Christian, not the Catholic, but the gentleman."[27]

THE "PROS" OF THE LIBERAL ARTS

On the other hand, there are, from an Augustinian point of view, at least three significant advantages to a liberal arts education. First, the liberal arts are useful in exposing superstition, false religion, and other forms of specious thinking. In Augustine's case, his familiarity with the discipline of astronomy helped him recognize the falsity of Manichean astrology, a discovery that ultimately led to his disillusionment with Manicheanism and his embrace of Christianity.[28] The liberal arts, of course, cannot prove what the true religion is, but even here Augustine was impressed that there is nothing in Christianity that can be proven false by the liberal arts.[29] The habits of intellectual acuity honed by the liberal arts gives one a nose for nonsense, and this is a disposition for which Augustine was forever grateful.

Second, the liberal arts can be enormously beneficial in helping to understand the Sacred Scriptures. This should come as no surprise, for as Augustine argues in *On Christian Doctrine*, the liberal arts are not invented by men but discovered by them, God being the author of the truths taught in a liberal education.[30] Nor is it surprising that there should be a compatibility between the Book of Nature and the Book of Revelation and that the former can be used to better understand the latter, since both have the same author. Hence, as Augustine famously puts it, if we Christians find pagans using the liberal arts, we should take them away as from "unjust possessors," just as the Hebrews despoiled the Egyptians on their exodus to freedom.[31] Book two of *On Christian Doctrine* may, in fact, be seen as a handbook on what tools from the liberal arts should be pilfered for Christian use, with Augustine essentially concluding that we should scarcely leave anything behind.

Third, although the liberal arts do not necessarily lead to that conversion of mind described in book seven of the *Confessions*, they are nevertheless instrumental in helping prepare the mind for such a breakthrough. This is the original function of the liberal disciplines as implied by Socrates in book seven of Plato's *Republic*,[32] and this is the reason why Augustine offers a detailed excursus of them in book two of his *On Order*.[33] As Augustine explains in his introductory letter to that dialogue, a multitude of impious and heretical errors arise from a lack of self-knowledge (i.e., from an ignorance of the incorporeal and intelligible nature of one's own cognitional operations), and that one promising balm to the "wound" caused by such ignorance is a liberal education.[34] This is a position from which Augustine never strays, not even in the *Retractations*. On the contrary, it is there that he repeatedly characterizes the liberal arts as that from which one can advance from the corporeal to the incorporeal.[35]

CHRISTIANITY, THE LIBERAL ARTS, AND
THE MODERN UNIVERSITY

Augustine's assessment of the liberal arts bears upon two of the modern university's most acute challenges. First, Augustine's stress that the liberal arts are constituted by truths capable of being discovered by the human mind provides a much-needed corrective to the identity crisis from which the humanities on most American campuses seem to be suffering. At but a slight risk of generalizing, the typical humanities department today has lost faith in the attainment of objective knowledge and is inclined instead to understand its methods and goals in terms of historicism or deconstructionism, neither of which admits the possibility of transcendent truth. Augustine's simple observation that fields such as logic and definition (grammar) are somehow eternal or transcendent and that they are there to be discovered with a little effort and acumen restores not only a *gravitas* but a sense of adventure and purpose to the educational endeavor: It frees us from the Sisyphean cycles of postmodernism and gives us a substantive, ever-new world to discover.

Moreover, if the liberal arts, properly practiced, are an alternative to the pointlessness or despair of relativism, they are also an invitation to a happier life. Stanley Fish, in the article to which I alluded earlier, makes much of the age-old distinction between the useful, servile arts that can build bridges and design software and the useless liberal arts, which he characterizes as "the splendid and supported irrelevance of humanist inquiry for its own sake."[36] This is true as far as it goes, but Fish never discusses the main reason why such splendor is so intrinsically satisfying, namely, that it opens a new vista free from society's aggressively growing number of wrong turns and dead ends about the "meaning of life," a vista oriented to becoming truly happy by living according to what is highest in us. Paradoxically, the useless can be most useful in the art of living well. Hence, W. E. B. DuBois' characterization of liberal education, which is perhaps the finest statement of its kind written by any American citizen:

> The riddle of existence is the college curriculum that was laid before the Pharaohs, that was taught in the groves by Plato, that formed the trivium and quadrivium, and is to-day laid before the freedmen's sons by Atlanta University. And this course of study will not change; its methods will grow more deft and effectual, its content richer by toil of scholar and sight of seer; but *the true college will ever have one goal—not to earn meat, but to know the end and aim of that life which meat nourishes.*[37]

This also brings us to an important corollary for any discussion on the American university, which is saddled with the added complication of living within a Lockean, consumerist paradigm that privileges pragmatism and productivity over "useless" contemplation and leisure. Though this paradigm is generally championed in the name of individual freedom and initiative, it all too easily leads to a lack of transcendence, which in turn elevates the importance of the State as the all-encompassing source and terminus of meaning. One safeguard against such a Hegelian encroachment of the State and an impoverishing reduction of man to a mere economic unit would be an institution that circumvents the problem by being dedicated to something altogether different. The best contribution the university can make to American life, in other words, might lie in its following a path different from the rest of America. And the beauty of this arrangement is that it is in accord with our American heritage. In the 1925 decision *Pierce v. Society of Sisters of the Holy Names of Jesus and Mary*—the only Supreme Court case, incidentally, ever quoted in a papal encyclical—the Court affirmed that

> the fundamental theory of liberty upon which all governments in this Union repose excludes any general power of the State to standardize its children. . . . The child is not the mere creature of the State; those who nurture him and direct his destiny have the right coupled with the high duty, to recognize, and prepare him for additional duties.[38]

Furthermore, just as Augustine's qualified endorsement of the liberal arts gainsays the claims of relativism, so too does his understanding of the liberal arts as pointing to intelligible, incorporeal realities upend the modern university's unspoken assumption that the more empirical or sense-based a branch of knowledge is, the more it is a true, objective science. If the typical American college student is a reliable gauge of current opinion, most people today think of the natural sciences and engineering as the primary fields from which to obtain "real" knowledge. Finishing in second place are the so-called social sciences, i.e., those disciplines that study partially non-empirical phenomena (such as human cognition, culture, and society) through the lens of a wholly empirical method of investigation,[39] all in an effort to capture some of the rigor and objectivity of their academic cousins. Try as they might, however, social scientists have never been able to dispel the suspicion that they are inventing their categories rather than discovering them, and so most students remain reluctant to refer to their sociology professor as a scientist in the same way that they would their professor of physics. The position of social science, however, is enviable in comparison with that of the humanities, which according to popular perception—and not entirely without warrant—is the leftover bin of higher education, the realm of the quirky, the bizarre, and maybe the interesting, but still the apogee in the constellation of learning from objective, verifiable reasoning. Hence something like theology, the study of the least material of realities, is seen as the apex not of knowledge, but of subjective opinion, personal experience or feeling, and very, very blind faith.

Intellectual conversion as detailed by Augustine, on the other hand, discloses a countervailing possibility, namely, that what is most real in *every* field of knowledge is not its material component but the immaterial laws and relations governing that component which are sought after by the scientist or scholar. Contrary to our common-sense expectations, Augustine holds that matter *qua* matter is shadowy stuff; it is the intelligible patterns intimated by those shadows, invisible to the eye but discernible to the mind alone, that we grasp in any authentic act of knowing. Therefore, *if* the humanities were done with an eye towards the intelligible, they would be neither a self-absorbed bohemianism nor an ideological and capricious dismembering of a text or idea: they would be a study of the real, perhaps even of the more real. Interestingly enough, Augustine's insight into the non-spatial, non-temporal dimension of reality is one which modern science for the past century has finally corroborated, for one of the lasting contributions of Einstein to our understanding of the universe is the realization that not all scientifically valid objects of inquiry fit within an absolute space-time continuum. Such an openness to the non-material oddly brings contemporary science more in line with the wisdom of the ancients than with the mechanistic determinism of Newton and his comet tail of disciples. Thus, as one scholar has observed, what took Augustine a lifetime to learn took modern science four centuries.[40]

Second, Augustine's stress on the limitations of the liberal arts poignantly reminds us of the need to foster both moral and religious excellence in every one of our students, for without these great goods, a liberal education is as likely to become a poison as a remedy. In the contemporary American context, this is no easy task. On the one hand, our longstanding commitment to individual freedom can easily be used to dismiss authority as an encroachment on one's autonomy; on the other, our more recent preoccupation with things such as diversity and multiculturalism leaves little room on the soapbox for any other kind of moral concern. The result of all this is that universities are eager to implement and then boast of those policies that agree with the progressive spirit of the age (which purportedly enhance the freedom of all) but reluctant, even frightened, to take a stand on anything that smacks of a supposedly traditional morality. Hence, while a dormitory forcing students to use unisex bathrooms or an administration hosting a freshmen orientation that encourages promiscuity draws little attention, an official promotion of say, modesty or chastity, is sure to bring down a maelstrom of protest. The last thing a major institution of higher learning would ever want said about it is that it still dares to act *in loco parentis*, a dreaded charge in a society where sometimes not even a mother and father are either eager or allowed to act as parents.

My point is not that this new morality is intrinsically evil but that when it becomes the principal object of attention it has the unfortunate effect of producing an ethical minimalism, one that does little to foster human beings who know, do, and love the good. This constriction of our moral taxonomy is evident in, say, the fact that one of the only kinds of sins we seem capable of recognizing today are sins against equality (sexism, racism, discrimination against homosexuals, etc.). It is evident also in our tendency to reduce all considerations of justice to the qualities of being nice, fair, and tolerant. Needless to say, to call for a complete reordering of one's passions, ambitions, and emotions, to call for an utter transformation of one's very being in the furnace of a love for the good, goes far beyond these relatively low and easy standards. Augustine's robust morality, however, is not only an arguably more beautiful thing than its contemporary counterpart: It is, he would argue, a necessary and indispensable companion to intellectual formation. Therefore, if a university is serious about the inculcation of knowledge, it must find within itself the courage to take seriously the moral condition of its students and not just the ethical idols of the day.

Finally, as Augustine mentions in *On Order*, the moral cultivation of the soul that is so beneficial to its intellectual growth cannot fully occur without the divine gifts of faith, hope, and charity.[41] For a liberal arts education to reach its full potential, then, religious as well as moral excellence is required, even though the liberal arts are not primarily ordered to the discovery of supernatural truth. There is no small dose of irony in this conclusion. For much of its history the Church, faced as it was with the dazzling competition of Greek and Roman wisdom, was forced to ask itself whether the knowledge of the heathen was compatible with the faith of the Apostles. Modern philosophical developments, however, have left us with a much different context. The implosion of the Enlightenment and the subsequent loss of confidence in reason have over the past century bred a suffocating cynicism about the mind's ability to discover anything but its own will to power. In a bizarre peripety that I suspect would have surprised Augustine, the secularism that liberated itself from Catholic Christianity in order to pursue objective truth is now enslaved to a skepticism that denies truth's very existence, while institutional Catholicism, purportedly the great enemy of rational inquiry, remains today as the only major international force that still affirms the human mind's capacity to grasp knowledge of the non-empirical. And so the question pressed upon us today is not, "Can the Christian faith live with the liberal arts?" but rather, "Can the liberal arts live without the Christian faith?"

NOTES

1. Augustine studied a number of the liberal arts in school, but he also tells us that he studied rhetoric, dialectic (logic), geometry, music, and arithmetic on his own (*Confessiones* 4.16.30).

2. *De ordine* 2.12.35; cf. Ilsetraut Hadot, *Arts liberaux et philosophie dans la pensée antique* (Paris, 1984), 101.

3. Cf. *Retractationes* 1.5.3. The *De grammatica* (now lost), the *De dialectica*, and the *De musica* were the only fruits of this project.

4. "The Last Professor," *New York Times* web log, January 18, 2009, fish.blogs. nytimes.com/2009/01/18/the-last-professor/.

5. *De ord.* 2.9.26.

6. *De ord.* 2.16.44.

7. *Conf.* 4.1.1.

8. *Conf.* 4.16.30.

9. *Retr.*, Prologus., 3. For the equation of *saeculares litterae* with the liberal arts, see Possidius, *Vita* 1.1.

10. *Retr.* 1.3.2.

11. *Retr.* Prol., 1.

12. *Retr.* Prol., 2.

13. *Conf.* 4.16.30.

14. *Conf.* 4.16.30.

15. *Conf.* 7.6.8 and 8.2.3, respectively.

16. *Conf.* 10.9.16.

17. *De ord.* 2.8.25.

18. *De ord.* 2.8.25, 2.20.52.

19. *De ord.* 2.20.52.

20. Cf. *De ord.* 1.11.31-32, 2.1.1.

21. "The Idea of a University," section IX, taken from *The Victorian Age: Prose, Poetry, and Drama*, 2nd ed., eds. John Wilson Bowyer and John Lee Brooks (New York: Appleton-Century-Crofts, 1954), 211.

22. *De ord.*, 2.11.30; *Soliloquia* 1.2.7.

23. Cf. *De ord.* 1.2.4.

24. Cf. *Conf.* 7.1.2, 7.10.16. Put differently, what Augustine discovered by reading the Platonists is that the mind is not the brain: it is a reality not confined to the parameters of space, time, and matter.

25. *Conf.* 7.10.16ff.

26. *Conf.* 4.16.31.

27. "The Idea of a University," op. cit.

28. *Conf.* 5.3.3.

29. *Conf.* 6.5.7.

30. Cf. *De doctrina Christiana* 2.32.50.

31. *De doctrina Christiana* 2.40.60.

32. *Rep.* 7.522c-535a.

33. *De ord.* 2.8.24-20.52.

34. *De ord.* 1.1.3.

35. *Retr.* 1.3.1, 1.5.3.

36. "Last Professor," op. cit.

37. From chapter 5, "Of the Wings of Atlanta," *The Souls of Black Folk*. Emphasis added.

38. Cited in part by Pope Pius XI in *Divini Illius Magistri* (1929), 37.

39. I say "partially non-empirical" for there are dimensions of human nature—and by extension, human things—that transcend space, time, and matter. Needless to say, applying to such a subject a methodology that takes its bearings from an empirical science is inherently problematic.

40. Bernard J. F. Lonergan, S.J., *Insight: An Inquiry into Human Understanding* (San Francisco: Harper & Row, 1978), xx–xxi.

41. *De ord.* 2.8.25.

10

Toward an American
Liberal Education

John Agresto

I write not to praise liberal education as much as to bury it. Actually, it died in bits and pieces starting a while ago, and it is only fit that its remains be interred. If there is any doubt about its demise, let's look at a few numbers. Today, the foremost major chosen by undergraduates is business, not English or history. Today, virtually a third of all university students are concentrated in just three areas, and none of them liberal arts: Business, education, and the health professions. Twice as many students study what are labelled "recreation, leisure, and fitness studies" as study philosophy and religion combined. More students attain bachelor degrees in "security and protective services" than in history. And in the race for majors, "consumer science" now edges out the physical sciences. And, let me add, none of these figures covers community colleges, which account for almost half of all of America's college students and where the liberal arts are even further submerged in a vast ocean of vocational, technical, and pre-professional training. Moreover, what was once seen as the most visible embodiment of the American collegiate ideal—the small residential liberal arts college—now accounts for about 5 percent of all institutions of higher learning in the country.

For most of us it is liberal education, not professional or technical training, that defines the heart of the educational enterprise. We say repeatedly that an education in the liberal arts, rather than an education in any specialty, produces men and women who are thoughtful, analytical, perceptive, well-spoken and "well-rounded." We hear the claim that students of the liberal arts turn out more sensitive, more understanding, even more virtuous. Why, we even hear it said that what we teach contributes to making our students "more fully human"—a claim that must grate fiercely in the minds of our more technically and professionally inclined colleagues. We repeat such things because, in part, we fancy them to be true and, in part, to make us feel better. Perhaps if we are no longer in the vanguard of education, at least we can take solace in being a self-consecrated though undervalued remnant. But a remnant we are.

Among the many, many reasons why the liberal arts, and especially that part of the liberal arts we call these days the Humanities, have fallen on such hard times, let me name at least three. I believe the liberal arts have an American problem (primarily a problem of utility), a moral problem, and, today, problem of self-understanding. Two of these—the moral problem and the American problem—are familiar stories, difficulties partly inherent in the nature of the enterprise itself. The problem of self-understanding, perhaps we might call it also the problem of postmodernism, is a wound inflicted on the body of the liberal arts that only the academy itself, in its infinite dopiness, could have done.

THE LIBERAL ARTS IN AMERICA

Let us begin with the matter of America. It is reported that, in 1691, the Rev. Dr. James Blair, founder and first president of the College of William and Mary, was rudely rebuffed by Sir Edward Seymour, Commissioner of the Royal Treasury. Blair, it seems, went to England to see if he could raise funds to start a university. When he said that he needed money so that a college could be started that might train young men for the ministry and thus help save souls in the New World, Seymour bellowed, "Souls! Damn your souls! Grow tobacco!" No doubt Blair would have gotten much the same response if he had said his college had hoped to improve men's intellect as well as save their souls.

As Americans, we have always been of two minds about the value of the liberal as opposed to the more useful and productive arts. On the one hand, by the time we established ourselves as a nation, we had, I believe, colleges of learning in every state. These were mostly religious institutions, to be sure, but each was devoted to improving the life of the mind as well as the salvation of souls. Philosophy, politics, theology and the sciences had a firm and active life in early America.

But there was always the other side. In his first Thanksgiving proclamation, for example, Washington noted the acquiring and diffusion of *useful* knowledge as a particularly worthy blessing of the Almighty. No mention was made in the proclamation of any particular gifts of liberal learning. In this he was echoing something of the words of the Constitution itself, which singles out the importance of "Science and useful Arts," as entitled to particular national protection.

Yes, we admire liberal education, we think it surely must be important; but more often as Americans we praise the useful arts and we reward the inventor and doer far more than the thinker. As we all know, the liberal arts began in the instruction of aristocratic men, free men, men who had leisure and who did not have to worry about working. We may have grandly expanded the idea, but "liberal education" still has at its core the old notion of learning for the sake of *knowing* and not learning for the sake of *use*.

But America is not a land of aristocratic leisure but of work. Yes, we do carve out a time for our children to have leisure—four years, sometimes more, to avoid the shop or the plow and go to university, to study and not to work: four years (if one goes to a good liberal arts institution) to study art and history and languages. But, after that, whether one studied the liberal arts or studied for a career, one begins to work. How odd might it seem to the citizens of antiquity that the freest people ever in all history devote their lives to work. But we do.

Now, as we've seen, most students do not take advantage of this offering; most *do* begin their careers in college studying what's most basic and needful for their future jobs. But, still, we take what are arguably the best of our students and invite them, nay encourage them, to spend time learning science and literature and history, subjects that they will never "put to use." How do we justify this?

In one way, these days, we justify it by a kind of sleight of hand. Perhaps we have to. We try to reassure everyone—citizens, parents, the students themselves—that *the liberal arts aren't disconnected from work at all!* Indeed, at their best, they're a kind of "pre-work," a preparation for all sorts of professions or careers.

Now, notice where this line of argumentation tends to put us. The argument that defends the liberal arts as the nursery of future success seems to imply that the education in what truly might be needful for our student's life comes *after* his liberal arts education: That it is the instruction of graduate school or the learning that comes with dedication to the job itself that actually does the real work of training, *for which the liberal arts were merely preparatory.* Contrary to all our occasional talk about the joy and value of liberal learning "for its own sake," often the best we can say of the liberal arts is that they *are* "preparatory"—that if they are not themselves professional they are surely "pre-professional." What else can we mean by saying that their value is in the fact that they have the ability to prepare us for a whole range of careers and occupations? And, in one stroke, we have changed the liberal arts into the new "servile arts," helpful training for the real education, the productive education, that comes later.

I have been in the business long enough to know that these arguments for the "usefulness" of the liberal arts are omnipresent in higher education. Collectively, they are the straw that contemporary liberal education grasps at because it not only has lost much of the ability to defend the liberal arts on their own terms but because it understands itself *compelled*, in the modern world, to say that these arts are, despite their nature and pedigree, truly productive after all. We live in America where, as I noted, we all work. If we were educating a leisured class, if we were educating plantation owners and nobility, or lords and landed gentry, we could rest content with notions of learning for its own sake. But this is America, and we cannot.

I say that in no way to slight or tarnish the greatness of America. In giving freedom to all and opportunity for all, we dismantled the old system of privilege by birth and reward the inventive, the productive, and the entrepreneurial. It was left for this age, and in large measure this nation, to build the great metropolises that house and give wages to millions, to plow the vast prairies that give sustenance to millions, to discover cures for diseases that give health and even life to millions. We have advanced the means of global communication and the near instantaneous transfer of information in ways that seem to deny the possible. We have produced abundance beyond the dreams of avarice and have become the wealthiest place in the history of the world by magnitudes. We have made it so that here, for the first time in human history, the words "poor" and "minority," rather than "poor" and "vast majority," are synonymous.

Prosperity, progress in the acquisition of material abundance, freedom from want, the elimination of disease, the exploration of the universe, vast networks of communication, comfort—these have been some of the goals, and the achievements, of this nation. But where in all this were the liberal arts?

I ask this knowing that progress in the material realm is not the business of the liberal arts and was never meant to be. But progress and production is the business of America, and it will help us understand something about the tenuous nature of liberal education in America if we can see how far from the goals of the country the liberal arts are, and why education in the more useful, more productive, arts is clearly so prized.

But our problems are deeper even than all that. Consider John Locke, truly one of the major founders of this country, talking about parents and children and Latin:

> Can there be any thing more ridiculous than that a father should waste his own money and his son's time in setting him to learn the *Roman language*, when at the same time he designs him for a trade, wherein he having no use of *Latin*, fails not to forget that little which he [studied], and which 'tis ten to one he

abhors for the ill usage it procured him? [Why should a child] be forced to learn the rudiments of a language which he is never to use in the course of [his] life, and neglect all the while the writing a good hand and casting accounts, which are of great advantage in all conditions of life, and to most trades indispensably necessary?

If you ask [parents] why they do this, they think it as strange a question as if you should ask them, why they go to church. Custom serves for reason, and has, to those who take it for reason, so consecrated this method, that it is almost religiously observed by them, and they stick to it.

If we consider the study of Latin as a paradigm of most liberal studies, it seems that the liberal arts have a double problem. They seem neither to be of value to the *individual,* nor of terribly much use to the *society.* The Latin grammar you studied or the historical dates you memorized or the difference between iambs and dactyls that the poetry professor kept talking about, all these are soon forgotten. And even if there's a remnant, a shadow of these left in the recesses of memory, so what? What good do they produce *for the individual?* If I aim to be a successful accountant, to learn and know *accounting* is, for me and my family, simply of greater value than knowing the kings of England and quoting the fights historical; surely better than memorizing which Latin preposition takes the ablative and which the accusative. Unless the liberal arts can show why and how they truly are of real value to the individual, and do it in ways that don't pretend that their true value is to be a preparation for the useful studies that will follow, students in this country will rightly look upon them as more or less a waste of time.

But that, as I say, is only the half of it. Say I have decided to devote my life to philosophy or to the study of antiquity or to critical theory. Why should any of my fellow citizens care? Or, to put it in terms I understood every day as a college president, why should society and its hardworking citizens give its resources toward helping a college where other people's children would read Aristotle or study Lobachevski? Toward what end and for what gain? That I now have a greater appreciation of a mathematical proof or that Suzy is studying Greek may well be exciting to me or to Suzy, but it hardly seems a great benefit to others or to the world at large.

The arts that most benefit society are not, it seems, the liberal arts, but the useful arts: doing, producing, growing, and selling. To study a trade, say electronics, or a profession, say dentistry, is, in our old language, "servile." To study philosophy or Attic Greek is liberal. But again: Why should the country care that Suzy is studying Greek? The well-trained electrician is a real benefit to hundreds of families, while the well-trained classicist may well be merely a curiosity. Even the fine arts, which give adornment to the world and enjoyment its people, have an easier case to make than the liberal arts.

So far, in any contest among the useful, the fine, and the liberal arts, it looks like the liberal arts are coming in third.

Now, neither John Locke nor I want simply to be petulant. Despite the magnitude of Locke's own liberal education, he wanted us to see *something* of the potential superiority of other varieties of education over liberal education. Custom, as he says, can no longer serve for reason; we have to be clear about what it is that the liberal arts can and cannot accomplish.

I know that, despite all our college catalogue talk, our grander purpose was always more than simply being an education that prepares young men and women to move up higher, into the professions of their choice. We once knew that we had more to offer than that. But I also know that all our old-fashioned talk about how we really are above it all, irrelevant to the pressing needs of society, has been killing us. If we are not relevant to the American project, the project of our fellow countrymen, then why should they any longer support us? And if we are relevant, we now had damn well be able to show how—and it better be more than "we'll help prepare you for your nice new career."

THE LIBERAL ARTS AND MORALITY

Beyond the issue of utility, there is what we need to look at second, the liberal arts and the moral problem. Take the poor position of parents these days. Parents have, from America's earliest days and before, always worried about what their children might *do* with a liberal education. But parental concerns today strike me as deeper than worries over job security and career advancement. If Johnny wants to major in business or Judy is eager to study engineering, parents not only have a sense of their children's future careers, but also perhaps something of their children's character. It is a fairly good bet that neither Johnny nor Judy will come home that first Thanksgiving from the college of engineering with spiked hair, body piercings, and a live-in companion replete with buttons urging the overthrow of all establishments. It is rare for finance majors to sit around denigrating common patriotism, ridiculing their parents' material aspirations, or raising up chants urging the demise of Western civilization. Yet none of this is rare for students studying anthropology, history, or literature, even—or especially—those at the more supposedly refined and advanced of our universities.

Let me take as my starting point some sentences from John Henry Newman on learning and morality, on knowledge and virtue:

> Knowledge is one thing, virtue another; good sense is not conscience, refinement is not humility. Philosophy, however enlightened, however professional, gives no command over the passions. . . .

> Taken by themselves, they [the liberal arts] do but seem to be what they are not; they look like virtue at a distance, but they are detected [i.e., exposed] by close observation, and on the long run.... Hence it is that they are popularly accused of pretense and hypocrisy, not I repeat from their own fault, but because their professors and admirers persist in taking them for what they are not, and are officious in arrogating for them a praise to which they have no claim.
>
> Quarry the granite rock with razors, or moor the vessel with a thread of silk; then you may hope with such keen and delicate instruments as human knowledge and human reason to contend against those giants, the passion and the pride of man.

Let us begin by taking take the view that the liberal arts aim indeed at *knowing* and that other parts of the curriculum aim at doing, making, or producing. This is the view that first characterized liberal education: Liberal education was an education that did not, purposefully did not, aim at any trade or profession. Now, as we have seen, the good that results from professional training is almost always a clear and tangible good. Virtually all of the vocational and technical arts aim at a good valued by our neighbors and countrymen— doctoring, house building, shoemaking, farming, pleading, fishing, nursing, homemaking, teaching children, physical therapy, car making, bookbinding. . . . That is, the non-liberal arts clearly aim at some good, or at least perceived good, and they each seem to want to improve the society they enter.

Moreover, while I think that the connection between the liberal arts and personal morality is tenuous at best, I do know, however, that it is the *non-*liberal arts that have the potential to make the doer, the practitioner, better! This is a hard thing to say, but one that seems to me simply true. Still, knowledge is not virtue and good sense is not conscience, as Newman reminds us.

I understand that it is conceivable that farming, nursing, doctoring, and pleading will sometimes be practiced for monetary enrichment. But I also know that the study of these arts very often stems from a desire partly rooted in a moral perspective: To help others live more comfortably, reduce their pain, cure their diseases, or have justice done to them. Even when they are not, even when the impetus for learning these skills stem from an initial desire wholly personal and even mercenary, often the *practice* of these trades and professions leads one to a greater consideration of the needs of others even when all we had in mind, originally, was satisfying ourselves. This is what de Tocqueville meant when he tells us how self-interest rightly understood often begins in mere self regard—we help others, for example, in the hope that they'll help us when we need them—but ends with our becoming accustomed, in time, to looking out for our neighbors' welfare more generally. This is something of what Aristotle meant when he talked about becoming "habituated" into virtue by the practice of moral acts.

So, consider the non-liberal arts in this context. Most often, these are the arts or skills that help you serve others in ways they find necessary or useful. Some of these, such as the training of a physician, are high arts indeed. But they are arts, skills, learned both for the sake of an object and for the benefit of others over and above oneself. One learns to be a doctor *primarily* to help the sick and only secondarily to help one's self. Despite both our modern-day cynicism and scattered examples to the contrary, we all know that this is true.

Now this is all very odd. It seems that what the liberal arts denigrate as "the servile arts" have within them a call to the service of others, and a drawing of us out of ourselves. I do not mean to say that service to others is the totality of virtue. Yet, in our everyday life, we recognize that virtue has something to do with our proper relation to others—to children, spouses, friends, neighbors, fellow countrymen, people in general, and perhaps to the world at large. Few are those who would rush to call a simply self-regarding act "virtue."

Now, how shall we discern the morality of the liberal arts? We know, as we said, that the liberal arts begin as the arts of freemen, of gentlemen, of men who had sufficient leisure not to worry too much about work. Gentlemen could indulge in that learning that neither aimed at production nor aimed at producing producers. "The useful arts," Aristotle tells us in the *Rhetoric*, are those which "bear fruit." The liberal arts are those "which tend to enjoyment . . . where nothing accrues of consequence" beyond the activity itself.

This means that there is a species of education that aims (in Aristotle's gentle phrase) at bearing fruit, and one which seems not to; one that aims at the making of goods and services for the benefit and enjoyment of others, and one that seems, shall we say, more personal. Even if we call them, harshly, the servile arts, these non-liberal arts seem beneficent, social, productive of good, helpful to society, and indeed helpful to the character of the doer himself. The liberal arts, conversely, seem private, inner-directed, and, to be blunt, a tad selfish. They seem not to aim at any public good and it's even unclear what private good they accomplish.

When the ancients first discussed the "good" of a liberal education they talked about it almost as the satisfaction of a necessary and natural impulse, a *personal* fulfillment. All men desire to know. Men and women have a capacity to wonder and to question which only knowing can satisfy. And the broader our yearning to know—to know about the heavens, about God, about nature and human nature, about justice and beauty and the sublime—the more we stray into the liberal and non-productive arts. So we start to study astronomy and music and logic—and those parts of our soul that yearn to learn begin to be satisfied. A gentleman, thus, can pursue knowledge not for what it can make or do but, as the phrase goes, "for its own sake."

I actually think that all of us sense the truth of this. We, each of us, find knowing pleasurable and satisfying, even if it leads to nothing beyond the knowing. Nevertheless, compared to shipbuilding or soldiering or medicine, the knowledge of the liberal arts again seems to begin and end with us. They seem inner-directed rather than publically beneficial. They may make us smarter; but can we argue from there that the liberal arts make us better? No one needs philosophy to be become courageous or friendly. Yes, prudence may need a kind of wisdom to help guide it; but, even there, it could certainly be the wisdom that comes from a combination of street smarts, experience, and a good disposition. So, again, how shall we argue that the liberal arts make us better? This is a very serious question. For, if the liberal arts do not make us better, or, through them help us make others better, why should we want them?

Let us take the liberal arts at their best. Let us say I have studied literature and I now know infinitely more about human nature than I would know through experience. I now have greater insight into the motives of others, their foibles, their psyches. I will now not be so easily fooled. I will be better able to tell the Desdemonas from the Iagos of this world. Perhaps I will learn science and study the secrets of nature. I will know a great deal about planets and heavenly motion, and, through the sciences, I will have insight into earthly bodies and their motions as well. I will study rhetoric and gain sweet, persuasive powers. I will learn the languages of others, and make their tongues my own. Am I, now, a better person? It could be argued that, through my studies and intellectual achievements, I am now better *empowered* to do good. If prudence is a virtue, I will know better how to achieve my goals rationally and intelligently. If justice is a virtue, I will know better, through my studies, how to give every man what he deserves. It is true: the liberal arts *are* a kind of empowerment to their possessor, and if used properly they will surely result in good.

Yet I'm not sure this leads us any closer to a moral defense. Indeed, so much depends on the character of the possessor. Rhetoric is a liberal art. And in the arsenal of a Lincoln or a Churchill it is a boon and blessing to the world. In the arsenal of an Alcibiades or Gorgias or Callicles or Caesar it is not. Rhetoric, perhaps all the liberal arts, would seem to be of value only *when attached to men and women of good dispositions*. But the liberal arts are fairly prostitute; they seem able and willing to bestow their charms on the good and bad alike. This may be a hard saying, but I doubt that it is a false one. Only if the liberal arts actually work to make us *better people* will their empowerment be praiseworthy. But, while we have noticed that they might satisfy a particularly human desire in us, the desire to know, we have yet to see that they make us better.

THE LIBERAL ARTS AND CIVIC VIRTUE

Perhaps we should approach the matter from a different side. Having seen that the vocational arts contribute to the good of society most directly and then, by indirection, to the betterment of the practitioner, perhaps the liberal arts have a connection not to our ethics as individuals but, rather, to society. More exactly, perhaps the liberal arts are the cultivators of a kind of *civic* virtue. We know how technology and agronomy and medicine and maybe even leisure studies help the society achieve its aims and desires; perhaps the liberal arts are themselves suffused with sufficient public spiritedness, sufficient civic virtue, as to help our culture satisfy the ends which it has set out for itself.

Indeed, it is exactly here where students and professors of the liberal arts often make claim. It is the practitioners of the liberal arts who are often the campus leaders in this or that movement for social betterment. Every demonstration, every rally, every strike, even every disruption tends to find not engineers, not chemists, not pre-med students, but those in the liberal arts and various allied disciplines leading the charge. While in older times a student of philosophy or languages might have barely enough time to begin to understand the world, today's students have, following Marx's dictum, gone past understanding the world to *changing* it. Is this not proof of their virtue, that they are willing to mobilize to make the world a better place? It was sufficient for the older liberal arts to hope, to try, to *understand* justice. It is left for the contemporary university to impose it, or at least their version of it.

Nonetheless, right now the question is not about any academically imposed vision of societal betterment but whether the liberal arts show any evidence of encouraging a general attachment *to the civic goals of the society*? This is, I believe, a perfectly legitimate question of all Americans to ask of their universities.

If that is what we mean by civic virtue, then it seems the answer from the academy is clear: It is *especially* the goals and foundations of the society that supports *them* that the modern liberal arts most question. Furthermore, it is not only the job of the liberal arts simply to question, but to criticize, very often to undermine, and finally to oppose.

So often, as the liberal arts and their practitioners see it, it is their duty to stand outside the society and often against the society and be critical questioners. For many, to be *critical* is the true work of the liberal arts; to be supportive of the goals and ambitions of the culture is to have sold out, and to have abandoned liberal education itself.

This view of liberal education—that the liberal arts are the questioners and critics of all accepted beliefs and orthodoxies—is so commonplace as to have become, itself, an orthodoxy, a foundational dogma of higher education. The claim today is that this view of the liberal arts as the great critics of cultural values is *of the essence* of the liberal arts: Was not Socrates, the original liberal artist, the one who showed them that their role is to confront, to question, and to expose the fallacies that everyone from low to high (but especially the high) thinks to be true? Was it not Socrates who taught that what most people thought correct, even their most cherished beliefs, were little more than foolish opinions, mere shadows on the cave wall—and that it was the job of the liberally educated to tell the rest that they believed in shadows? Was it not Socrates who taught the young to call into question everything that society believed—to call into question whatever was taught by inherited tradition or by religion or by parents or the ruling powers? The "virtue" of the liberal arts is not to affirm but to doubt.

I have to say that, call it what you will—even give it fancy academic labels like "the hermeneutics of suspicion" or the hermeneutics of rejection—this understanding of the liberal arts as *naturally* the opponents and critics of whatever society they occupy is so narrow, so diminished, and, in many cases, so self-destructive a view of the liberal arts that I believe that the whole enterprise of liberal education cannot again prosper without its significant re-thinking.

The liberal arts have become so dogmatic in this view that they cannot even talk any longer of "thinking"—the rage is now "critical thinking." And this is also why it has been so easy to politicize the liberal arts in today's world—their aim is not to wonder, not to understand, not to explain but, simply, *to be critical*. The questioning of all orthodoxies and the destruction of all idols has become, today, the liberal arts' true work.

Given this, it is hardly surprising that what were once traditional and conservative disciplines have now been transformed and radicalized. If "deconstructionism" seems the synecdoche for all of academic post-modernism it is because "tearing down" fits in so nicely with the dogma that proclaims those in the liberal arts to be the anointed antagonists of all orthodoxy.

This is also why the liberal artists so often have a smugness and pride about them: What else should one feel but pride when you've managed to degrade the revered, expose the ignorance of the supposedly wise, and show the shallowness of so many cherished beliefs?

So to ask a question of the civic virtue of the liberal arts is to ask a question that seems nonsensical on its face: civic virtue necessitates support for the civic project of fellow citizens; but the job of the liberal artist is to criticize and question, not support. Or so we are constantly told.

This supercilious attitude of subversion and criticism leads most naturally into what has clearly been the last wave of attack against the work and promise of the liberal arts. In America, it started in the late 1960s at Cornell, Wisconsin, Columbia, and Berkeley. It took root in the 1970s with the general acceptance of the various new "studies" within higher learning—Women's studies, Black studies, Chicano studies, and Gay studies. It reached something of a peak in the late 1980s with the furor over Stanford and the revision of its semi-great books core offering called "Western Culture" to something more diverse, more sensitive to the desire of minorities to gravitate to their own studies, and to undermine the study of what came dismissively to be called "the West." And it was strengthened and given theoretical cover by the rise not only of a philosophy of multiculturalism but of all the theories that had knowing "culture" rather than knowing objects more transcendent at their core.

All this culminated in the widespread regime of political correctness, a regime that not only brooks no disobedience, it tolerates no questioning. In that regard, what happened to the hapless Larry Summers—at what was once thought to be the flagship American university—is definitive. And, in tolerating no questioning, no inquiry into significant matters if the matter can be deemed disquieting, liberal education was finally killed. It was not killed by relativism, exactly, nor by nihilism. It was killed by a deadly mix of strongly held beliefs—the thought that all thought is epiphenomenal, bound by its culture and unable to break through the power relations prevalent at the time; that, therefore, no thought is truly trans-cultural or universal in nature; that while nothing of great value can be salvaged from the past—dead white males have nothing to say to the diversity of sexes, life-styles, or ethnic and economic minorities that make up today's world—we can learn one thing: that the history of the West has been the history of oppression; that it is the obligation of today's academy to support the liberation and empowerment of those formerly oppressed; and that any attempt to pretend that the academy should be non-political in this regard is not true, was never true, and they in the post-modern Humanities have no shame in announcing it: Teaching is Politics by another name.

THE RESURRECTION OF THE LIBERAL ARTS?

So, if you, or we, wanted to revive, resurrect the liberal arts, where would we begin? We would have to begin at the beginning. We would have to deny the post-modern supposition that knowledge is cultural while acknowledging the importance of the knowledge of culture. We would have to reassert, or, more accurately, show that truth is a possibility universally. That is, we'd have to show that the old promise of the liberal arts—that it can help us have knowledge of the most important things through reason and reflection—is still possible. We would have to show the world that what we study and teach truly are important matters, matters of real human significance. We have to find ways of showing that while the liberal arts may not be "of use" that they still can be "of value" and then demonstrate what that value might be, and not just pretend that it's obvious. We have to stop looking down on the schools of business and engineering and nursing and what have you and recognize that, in this country, they do good and moral work. We have to understand that, if we no longer have suitors, it is because we are no longer lovely. We have to stop with the smugness and haughty attitude that we're well-rounded and all others in the academy who teach practical things are truncated or deformed. Arrogance is unbecoming a body that's dead. We have to understand that we weren't killed by vocationalism or science or the infatuation with the modern or by commercialism or materialism, but we killed ourselves. We have to understand that the nature of the liberal arts is not found in opposition, not found merely in criticism or rejection, but in wonder. We are not Socrates because we call all things into question; anyone can do that. We imitate Socrates when we look at the universe and marvel—when we ask our authors to tell us what they know and ask them to raise us up, not when we think we know what makes them tick or motivates them or where they so obviously went wrong. Finally, once again to live and even to prosper, we will have to show that there can actually be an *American* liberal education, one that rightly honors what America rightly honors, one that helps it understand itself and the principles that undergird it, one that has regard for the qualities of our fellow citizens and has the desire to improve their lot and not merely criticise it, one that makes us smarter in areas that really matter. That is, an American liberal education that satisfies the Founders' hopes that this nation's citizens would be so knowledgeable about history, so cognizant of their duties, so intelligent about the alternatives, and, above all, so thoughtful regarding the principles that give life to the country, that liberty and democracy might both survive and prosper.

Index

About the Editor and Contributors

Bradley C. S. Watson is Professor of Political Science at Saint Vincent College, where he holds the Philip M. McKenna Chair in American and Western Political Thought and is Co-Director of the Center for Political and Economic Thought. He is also Senior Scholar at the Intercollegiate Studies Institute and a Fellow of the Claremont Institute. He has held visiting faculty appointments at Princeton University and Claremont McKenna College. He has authored or edited many books, including *Civic Education and Culture* and *Living Constitution, Dying Faith: Progressivism and the New Science of Jurisprudence*. He has published in both professional and general interest forums such as *Armed Forces and Society, Claremont Review of Books, The Intercollegiate Review, Modern Age, National Review*, and *Perspectives on Political Science*. He was educated in Canada, Belgium, and the United States, and holds advanced degrees in law, philosophy, and political science.

John Agresto currently serves as Provost of the American University of Iraq in Sulaimani. He is also a member of the University's Board of Trustees and chair of the Academic Affairs Committee. Between August 2003 and June 2004, he served as Coalition Provisional Authority Senior Advisor to the Ministry of Higher Education and Scientific Research in Baghdad. In this capacity he assisted the ministry with physical rehabilitation, intellectual renewal, curricular reform, and the opening up of Iraq's universities to the outside world. His book on the situation in Iraq, *Mugged by Reality: The Liberation of Iraq and the Failure of Good Intentions*, was published in 2007. He previously served as President of St John's College, Santa Fe and is widely published in the areas of politics, law, and education. He has also taught at the University of Toronto, Kenyon College, Duke University, and the New School University. He has been the Lilly Senior Research Fellow in Liberal Arts at Wabash College and a Senior Fellow at the James Madison Program in American Ideals and Institutions at Princeton University.

William B. Allen is dean and professor emeritus at Michigan State University. He was 2008–09 Visiting Senior Scholar in the Matthew J. Ryan Center for the Study of Free Institutions and the Public Good at Villanova University. He has also served on the National Council for the Humanities and as Chairman and Member of the United States Commission on Civil Rights. He was recently the Ann and Herbert W. Vaughan Visiting Fellow in the James Madison Program in American Ideals and Institutions at Princeton University. He is an expert on liberal arts education—its history, importance and problems. He published most recently *Rethinking Uncle Tom: The Political Philosophy of H. B. Stowe*, and *George Washington: America's First Progressive*.

Michael P. Foley holds a degree in systematic theology from Boston College and is an Associate Professor of Patristics in the Great Texts Program at Baylor University. He is the editor of *Saint Augustine: Confessions*, trans. F. J. Sheed, 2nd ed. (Indianapolis, Indiana: Hackett Publishing, 2006) and the author of numerous articles on political philosophy, St. Thomas More, St. Thomas Aquinas, Catholic liturgy, and film criticism. He is currently working on a four-volume translation of and commentary on St. Augustine's Cassiciacum dialogues.

Gary D. Glenn is distinguished Teaching Professor Emeritus of Political Science at Northern Illinois University. He has published numerous articles and book chapters and delivered many papers and lectures. He writes on the history of political philosophy and American political thought. He has received both of the campus wide teaching awards given by Northern Illinois University: the Excellence in Undergraduate Teaching Award (1995) and Presidential Teaching Professor Award (2000). He is a member of the National Council for the Humanities. He received his B.A. from Loras College and his M.A. and Ph.D. from the University of Chicago.

Susan E. Hanssen is associate professor of history at the University of Dallas, where she teaches American and Western civilization as part of a liberal arts great books core curriculum. She holds her doctoral degree in British and American history from Rice University and has published on

G. K. Chesterton and the development of the idea of "the English-speaking peoples" during the two World Wars. She is interested in the development of national, regional, and religious identity and the role that education plays in maintaining a strong sense of cultural identity.

Mark C. Henrie is Senior Vice President and Chief Academic Officer at the Intercollegiate Studies Institute. He is the editor of the *Intercollegiate Review* and executive editor of *Modern Age* and the *Political Science Reviewer*. He is the author of *A Student's Guide to the Core Curriculum* and editor of *Doomed Bourgeois in Love: Essays on the Films of Whit Stillman* and *Arguing Conservatism: Four Decades of the Intercollegiate Review*. His articles and reviews have appeared in numerous journals. He was valedictorian at Dartmouth College and holds graduate degrees from the University of Cambridge and Harvard University. He resides in West Chester, Pennsylvania, with his wife Claudia and their five children.

Peter Augustine Lawler is Dana Professor of Government at Berry College in Georgia. He is also executive editor of the acclaimed scholarly quarterly *Perspectives on Political Science,* and was a member of President Bush's Council on Bioethics. He has authored or edited 12 books, including *Homeless and at Home In America, Stuck With Virtue, Aliens In America,* and *Postmodernism Rightly Understood*. His *Modern and American Dignity* is forthcoming from ISI Books. He has published over 200 articles and essays in a wide variety of publications and has spoken at over 60 colleges and universities. He was the 2007 winner of the Richard M. Weaver prize in scholarly letters.

William Mathie teaches political philosophy in the Political Science Department at Brock University in Canada and was the founding director of Brock's Great Books/Liberal Studies Program, an undergraduate program modeled on the program at St. John's College. He studied under George Grant in Canada and Leo Strauss at the University of Chicago. He has published essays in political philosophy on Thomas Hobbes, Aristotle, Tocqueville, George Grant, and Abraham Lincoln. He has also written on liberal education in the writings of Tocqueville, Adam Smith, Cardinal Newman, and Allan Bloom.

Father James V. Schall, S.J., has interests in classical and medieval political philosophy, natural law, Christian political philosophy, and the nature of political philosophy. His books include: *Reason, Revelation, and the Foundations of Political Philosophy, Another Sort of Learning, At the Limits of Political Philosophy,* and *Jacques Maritain: The Philosopher in Society.*

He also writes two columns, "Sense and Nonsense," in *Crisis* magazine and "Schall on Chesterton," in *Gilbert Magazine.*

Peter W. Wood is president of the National Association of Scholars. He is the author of *A Bee in the Mouth: Anger in America Now* (2007) and of *Diversity: The Invention of a Concept* (2003). He previously served as a college provost and a professor of anthropology. His essays on American culture and higher education have appeared in *National Review Online, Partisan Review, Minding the Campus, The Claremont Review of Books, The American Conservative, Society* and other journals.